Modern Mothering

Modern Mothering

What Daughters Say They Need from Their
Mothers Regarding Sexual Development
and Its Impact on Their Self Worth

JOYCE T. MCFADDEN

MODERN MOTHERING
What Daughters Say They Need from Their Mothers
Regarding Sexual Development and Its Impact on Their Self Worth

Copyright © Joyce T. McFadden 2018

First published in 2011 under the title
Your Daughter's Bedroom: Insights for Raising Confident Women
Published by Palgrave Macmillan
in the United States—a division of St. Martin's Press LLC.
ISBN 978-0-692-16164-7
Library of Congress Control Number: 2018908779

Library of Congress Cataloging-in-Publication Data
    McFadden, Joyce T.
        Modern Mothering : What Daughters Say They Need from
        Their Mothers Regarding Sexual Development and Its Impact
        on Their Self Worth
    Joyce T. McFadden
        240 p.
    Includes Index
    ISBN 978-0-692-16164-7
        1. Women—Sexual behavior. 2. Mothers—Sexual behavior.
3. Daughers—Sexual behavior. 4. Sex instruction. 5. Mothers and daughters—Psychology. I. Title.

Cover Design by Phoebe Morrison
Cover Illustration by Joana Avillez
Interior Design by Cindy Butler

Printed in the United States of America

For Olivia
The privilege of loving you has been my resurrection.

Contents

Forward

*M*odern *Mothering* was originally published by Palgrave Macmillan under the title *Your Daughter's Bedroom: Insights for Raising Confident Women* and marketed with a hot pink bra on the cover. From the time it was proposed I felt the cover didn't accurately reflect the manuscript. But as a first time author, I had a standard contract and despite my objections and those of my literary agency, Manus and Associates, I was contractually bound to accept Palgrave's marketing department's choice of title and cover art. For years this made me uncomfortable. It was frustrating having a book I was proud of represented by a cover I wasn't. So this year I finally made the decision to ask Palgrave to revert the rights to me so I could reissue it with a new title and cover, and they graciously agreed. With the exception of this Forward nothing in the book has changed. That being said, our national climate has. With the advent of the #MeToo movement, the Women's March, and further erosion of reproductive rights, I believe the stories told by women and girls in this book are more pertinent, moving and necessary than ever.

For their support in getting *Modern Mothering* all dressed up and ready to go I thank Chris Davis, Bill Gaden, Dan Schwartz, and Nicole Passage. A respectful nod to The Wing for getting me fired up enough to actually go through with the rights reversal. Thanks also to the lovely Tawni Bannister for the author photo, and to Cindy Butler for the beautiful manuscript design. Much gratitude to Phoebe Morrison for designing the perfect cover and for fitting in all the content while still having it look clean and bright. And because she was the only artist I wanted and because I might not have done it without her signing on, my deepest appreciation to Joana Avillez. Whenever I see her illustrations I want to jump into them and hang out with her characters. Talking about female sexuality can freak people out, and I wanted women to be soothed by seeing themselves in the mothers and daughters on the cover. They show us how conversations of *all* kinds occur naturally in the routine of our days, and it's those little moments that shape and strengthen us, and have the power to forge a bond like no other.

Acknowledgments

*D*uring my analytic training one of my supervisors, Peter Zimmermann, said to me when I told him how much I love working with my clients: "It's a privilege to have someone sit and tell you their story." To all of my clients, past and present, female and male, my training taught me how to listen, but what I know of the finest of human nature and compassion has come through you. Everything you've taught me runs through each of these pages and I thank you for all of it. To the women who participated in the Women's Realities Study, I consider this book a gift from you to today's women and the girls who represent the next generation. I wish I could have had a cup of coffee with every single one of you as your stories rolled in, to tell you in person how indebted to you I am, and to let you know that even though we don't know each other, each of you holds a unique place in my heart. To my agent, Dena Fischer, this is *our* book. You are the greatest—you put five years of your life into this project and not only did we get to put women's unforgettable voices in print, we built a dear friendship to remember it by. Thank you for everything you did to get it out into the world. To Penny Nelson and Jillian Manus of Manus and Associates, my deepest appreciation for having my back in defense of what I believe in. To my editor, Luba Ostashevsky, I'm so fortunate this book ended up in your hands. Thank you for protecting the manuscript's integrity and for the ways you elevated it as a contribution to the social sciences. Writing it under your guidance gave me the kind of experience writers dream of, and I am forever grateful. Thanks also to Laura Lancaster for your help and for your welcoming smile when I first walked into Palgrave Macmillan's offices. To Jillian Straus, thank you for your faith in my research and for helping me get it packaged and ready for sale. The momentum you brought was perfect. A special thank you to Mary Ellen McGahey for the fabulous Women's Realities website photo you shot in your garage in Shelter Island with all of these cool women in it, each of whom I also thank: Robin Streck, Thelma Brathwaite, Mary Beth Lamond, Elaine DeFalco, Liana Tutino, Collette Tutino, Olivia McFadden, and Karen Roser. Thanks to Carole Van Almelo for creating my website, showing me oh so patiently how to use it, and for designing it to be easy for women to use; thanks to Frank Lopresti at NYU for teaching me, over polenta at Union Square Café, how to get my research off the ground and running, and to Toby Buloff for your legal advice. To the friends and colleagues who have been involved in this project from the beginning: First and foremost thanks to Karen Roser and Anne Tierney for all those Monday-night dinner conversations in Anne's apartment. If it hadn't piqued your enthusiasm my resolve may have fizzled; thanks to Gordon Powell for your general spectacularness, for reading, offering your expertise, and for the time you put into being there for me; and to Carole Symer, thank you for standing by my side from the time this book was only the seed of an idea for a workshop. I'm grateful for every gracious conversation you held out to me whenever you came across material for my research. Thanks also to everyone who came to my think-tank night or other events: to Debbie Klein—one of the finest women ever—and to Dianne Langona, thank you for the ideas both of you offered, and to Louisa Waber for being such a true and constant friend. Thanks to Aviva Rohde for the encouragement that made expressing my ideas in writing less scary, and for your kindness as new friends, I thank Anne Sikora and Eric Simonoff.

My sincere gratitude to the New York Hospital doctors who helped me disseminate the study by letting me invite your patients to participate in it: to Holly Andersen, Laura Fisher, and, for going above and beyond in your support, pediatrician extraordinaire Barbara Landreth; thanks also to Judy Wenger for being the champion of women's health and sexuality that you are. Thank you to the *Huffington Post*—a big fat kiss to Chris Davis for the opportunity to write and be read, and to Jessica Wakeman and Anya Strzemien for featuring me, especially Anya, for allowing me to reach out to *Huffington Post* readers who were interested in being in the study. For helping me put forward the voices of women who too often go unheard, I thank Jo Brown and the women in the 92nd Street Y Senior Program, the residents of the Brighter Tomorrows domestic violence shelter of Long Island, and the Native American women of the Shinnecock Indian Nation. Thanks also to the students and alumnae of Colgate University for your participation, to Ronnie Sharpe and the Southern Marin Mother's Club, and to Julie Carles and The Yarn Company. A heartfelt thank you to Nancy Turcotte for helping me reach women I may not have reached otherwise. Thanks to Jackie Dunphy, who, in the beginning when I thought I wasn't going to be able to conduct the study because I couldn't afford to mail out pounds of paper questionnaires, looked at me with the pity and incredulity someone of my computer illiteracy deserves and said, "Joyce: Do it on *the internet.*" To my oldest girlfriend, Nancy Gaden, thank you for your very fine mind and heart and the incredibly insightful contributions you made in crystallizing the most important themes in the book. I'm lucky to have had you in my life for this long and I think you should leave Boston and move to New York. Much appreciation to Jenna Osiason for taking my postcards to hand out, offering to help me find lecture spaces, and supporting me through two book proposals. Thanks to my lovely friend Jane Umanoff for everything, and to Peter Zimmermann for your professional endorsement of me in an effort toward getting my study recognized. Thank you to Douglas Katz for being such a thoughtful and discerning reader—your humor and the way you put things always makes me see something anew. Thanks to Bettina

Voltz for your child psychology wisdom, and to Laurie Gordon for the incisive editing that got me unstuck when I needed it most. And for being generous with me before we even met, I thank the refreshingly inspiring Esther Perel. For helping me in a pinch and taking my author photo in your beautiful home at the last minute I thank my warm and talented friend Philippe Cheng. To my soul mate of 40 years, Bill Love, I thank you for more than I can do justice to here. To my dear friends Bill Gaden, Peter Foley, and Lisa Jacobs, thank you for your long-standing encouragement and friendship, and the joy of having it routinely unfold around great food—with a special nod to Peter for doing double duty by providing your professional expertise. To the girls in my life—most, but not all of whom are now on the cusp of womanhood—girls, who, alongside your mothers, I have watched grow as you brought us joy giggle by giggle, conversation by conversation—thank you. And lastly, to Thaddeus McFadden—thank you for always being fully behind my career, and, for the last 25 years, encouraging me to write. Writing this book at the desk you bought for me all those years ago will stand out as one of the greatest experiences I will ever have. Mostly, though, thank you for being a father who respects and encourages his daughter's vitality in *all* areas of her life.

Introduction
_____

A Cautionary Tale

*A*nne was an up-and-coming chef in her early thirties when she came to see me for grief therapy. Her mother had died of ovarian cancer a year earlier and Anne was unsettled because in addition to feeling the loss, she was carrying around a lot of anger.

Each session, she would come in and sit very still in the center of the couch. This isn't unusual for someone in mourning, but over time, in much of what she would share, it became apparent that the way she carried herself was older than her grief. I remember being struck by the discrepancy between her incredibly bright and engaging eyes and the recurring image I had of her walking through her life with her arms glued to her sides. Over the course of her treatment the following story emerged.

All her life Anne had been the "good girl" because her mother, although she never called her a slut, treated her as if she were. The innuendo had been pervasive, and Anne recounted many memories of feeling dirty and ashamed, confused, alone, hurt, and let down as a result of her mother's treatment of her. When I asked her to tell me about an episode that illustrated her feelings, she immediately recalled a time shortly after her family had moved from Chicago to San Francisco and she was the new girl in junior high school. Her mother, noticing two neighborhood boys riding their bikes down the street, turned to Anne and asked in a nasty tone, "What did you do to make those boys ride their bikes by our house?" Anne's reaction was to feel guilty, "even though I hadn't done anything. I was caught off guard because she'd turned on me out of the blue...and I remember being sure to dress plainly when I got ready for school the next day even though I certainly didn't own anything provocative." As she was finishing telling me this story, she grew quiet and started to tear up.

I asked her what she was thinking that made the tears come, and she said, "It's ridiculous. I'm a 32-year-old woman and I still dress plainly when I go out so I don't draw attention to myself. I don't wear the things I wish I could. And it doesn't matter whether I'm going to be out with men or my girlfriends."

Even though her mother hadn't taught her about desire, menstruation, or anything to do with reproductive health, Anne had received an ongoing tutorial, sometimes indirect and sometimes blatant, on the "badness" of sexuality. For years Anne had tried to talk about female issues with her mother—menstruation, dating, birth control—in part to prove her status as a "good girl" and in part to get valuable information on growing up, but her mother kept that door firmly shut. By her sophomore year in college Anne gave up trying.

Shortly after her mother's death, in an emotional evening at the kitchen table, her father let it slip that Anne's mother had had an abortion before they were married and an affair when Anne was in high school. This news completely shocked Anne, and the more she thought about it the more furious she became. When I asked her to tell me more about what made her angry, she said in exasperation, "The whole time she was out there living her life, but she expected me to be a nun!"

As for her feelings about her mother's secrets, Anne, now a married woman herself and well aware of the minefields couples walk through, was deeply affected by these revelations. She was surprised to learn her mother had had such complex life experiences, especially since she had always felt sad that her mother had seemed so closed off. And rather than judging her mother for her experiences, she felt disappointed that they'd never had the chance to know each other as adult women who lived real lives and faced real emotional dilemmas. Anne's anger wasn't connected to her mother's sexual choices; it was connected to her mother's inability to love her and see her for who she was, especially once Anne began to develop sexually and sought her support. Instead of her mother's experiences softening her to be more compassionate and understanding toward her daughter, Anne had felt cast out of the mother-daughter bond whenever they treaded subjects that were even tangential to sexuality. "All I wanted was for us to be close," was something Anne would frequently say in session. But her mother had been so engulfed by issues of her own sexuality that she wasn't able to see what her daughter needed most from her: an ongoing sense of belonging to the same gender.

Together we explored the possibility that, albeit in hostile ways, perhaps Anne's mother had been trying to protect her from experiencing the kind of sexual shame she herself likely felt. But in doing so, she had merely exchanged passing down one type of shame for another.

We also explored the extensive ripple effect created by the tension with her mother around female sexuality, one that had set a cold tone for a good part of their relationship and left Anne feeling depressed and misunderstood. As a by-product of her mother's unwillingness to engage on topics related to sexuality, Anne repeatedly felt trapped in an ongoing internal battle between obeying the way her mother had raised her and following her own instincts. Because of this, she gradually came to feel a lack of normal and healthy entitlement to be true to herself. It influenced how she felt in her body, and it heightened her physical tentativeness and the shame and guilt she felt whenever she tried to listen to her own sexual voice. It created an unsettling discomfort whenever attention of any kind was paid to her, even going so far as making her reluctant to raise her hand in class. It influenced the way she dressed, the things she kept secret from her girlfriends, and later the way she judged or envied other women. It influenced the activities she felt comfortable participating in and the difficulty she had in speaking up to offer her opinion throughout her academic and professional education. It left the impression that if she ever needed help she shouldn't dare ask. It influenced her choice of a husband to whom she wasn't sexually attracted, and a career in which she took care of others by feeding them on a schedule that exhausted her and took away from her time for herself. Lastly, it influenced her decision never to turn to her mother when there were issues in her own marriage. One of the most powerful declarations she made during therapy was, "I feel like my mom raised me to be alienated from myself."

The distance Anne felt from *her* true self was compounded by the distance she felt from her *mother's*. Her grief was complicated by her realization that, in the end, she and her mother were, to a great extent, strangers.

* * *

I begin with Anne's story because at first sight it's merely an account of a mother's impact on her daughter's sexuality. Yet that simplification hides a little-discussed fact in our society: a mother's impact on her daughter's sexual sense of self will affect her in ways that extend far beyond sexuality. When a daughter is raised to believe that something as natural as her sexuality is shameful and should be hidden, her ability to reveal and be true to herself in other areas of her life will be compromised. A mother's sense of self doesn't exist in a vacuum, and Anne's story exposes how a mother's feelings about her own sexuality can pervade every aspect of her daughter's sense of self *over her lifetime*. This is clear in all of the ways Anne describes how the legacy of her mother's shame made her feel restricted in her body, her relationships, her emotional, academic, and professional life, and her choices. Whenever I think of the lives of these two women and the shame weaving through them, my heart goes out to both of them.

A major voice in feminist studies, Carol Gilligan, the founder of the Harvard Center for Gender and Education, has spoken on the unhealthy patterns that pass from mother to daughter. She argued that a girl's valuing of herself is stunted when it's not joined and strengthened by the mother. In other words, if a mother doesn't value and protect certain qualities in herself and in her daughter, it will be difficult for her daughter to value and protect them in herself. If this pattern of undermining isn't interrupted it will continue into the next generation. Gilligan speaks to the power of conscious awareness in changing this, saying, this is where "the wisdom and the knowledge of psychology comes in and says, this doesn't have to repeat, you can break this cycle."[1]

Anne's relationship with her mother allows us a glimpse inside how women might unwittingly pass down feelings of sexual shame to their daughters. But what's promising about their story is that it can inspire us as mothers to reconsider the importance of encouraging our daughters to feel connected to us around sexuality, sensuality, and erotic life: *to bestow on ourselves and our daughters our own permission to be whole.*

Barbara Marcus, a psychologist at the Yale University School of Medicine, identifies the same dynamic between women that spans families and generations. She writes that a mother is "rarely seen as a girl's source of identification as a vibrant, sexually desirous woman." When a mother conveys pride in the sexual and reproductive capacities of her own body, and an appreciation of sensuality and passion in her life, she invites her daughter to experience the same as she matures. This sharing of a full sense of self enhances the mother-daughter relationship not only when daughters are young, but it also creates closeness as mothers and daughters go through adulthood together.[2]

There is growth and wellness to be gained in valuing and strengthening our daughters' sexuality as well as our own—to grant *each other* permission to be whole—and it is incumbent on us as mothers to make that happen.

But doing this seems challenging given the divisions society imposes on us. The Madonna/whore or good girl/bad girl split is nothing new, and it can still make us feel we have to choose between one or the other, not to mention the worry of being perceived as one or the other. I propose that in addition to looking with fresh eyes at this unnatural split, we also need to examine the forced, rigid division between girl and woman, and daughter and mother. These divisions don't make room, they limit it. The mother-daughter relationship isn't static—it changes over the years. And we don't really cross a line into being sexual or becoming a woman. It is a gradual process. Even though we can say that birth is the demarcation of mother and daughter, that menstruation marks the start of reproductive function, and that the loss of virginity is the point at which sexual behavior deepens, there is no such border in the development of our sense of *who we are* and *what our relationships mean to us*. We don't just explode into our personality one day, nor do we explode into our sexuality. And we don't stay locked into only one way of being a mother or daughter. It all unfolds gradually as we piece together what ends up being our lives, relationship by relationship, experience by experience. Unfortunately, as women we go through our lives getting negative feedback on our sexuality, and we need to untangle our daughters and ourselves from the emotional restriction that comes from this lack of support. We as mothers have to stop participating in sustaining the lore that females need to be quarantined in sexual or nonsexual zones. Mothers can help dissolve these boundaries, and the first step in doing that is to acknowledge that our daughters' sexuality exists on the very same continuum as our own. The easiest way for us to do that is by listening to our most valuable resource: our own stories.

We learn how to be women in the context of other women. But we miss out on so much we could be learning from each other because we keep certain parts of ourselves hidden, sometimes even from those we love. And understandably so; it's hard to make decisions about what private things to reveal, because we fear the penalties of being judged or humiliated, or running the risk of losing relationships. But it's usually the stories we guard the most ardently that bring us the greatest emotional release or that have the most effect on others when we share them.

This book is full of such stories. Some are taken from my 25 years of practice as a psychoanalyst, some from public examples in our culture, and some from my private life as a woman and the lucky mother of a fifteen-year-old daughter. But this book is primarily built on what the hundreds of women in my Women's Realities Study (explained in the following section) had to say. It is a collection of their narratives, kept anonymous and in their own words. These narratives will allow us to look into their innermost worlds and their most deeply intimate experiences, expressed with raw honesty. I hope as women read this book that connections to your own lives will emerge that will advance your appreciation of the realities of what it's like to be female in our society.

My client Anne's experience shows us the dangers of what can happen to our daughters and our relationships with them when the very things we do to protect them end up harming them. If we try to insulate them by suppressing their sexuality we risk impairing their ability to thoroughly engage in life. As mothers we can't erase all of the unfair or frightening things our daughters might encounter. But by creating space in the mother-daughter dynamic for the validation of female sexuality, we're promoting a feminist ideal of fairness between the sexes, improving the quality of our relationships with our daughters, and creating an environment where everything we face as women can be easier and less lonely.

Even though Anne's mother made choices on which society might look askance, it wasn't that piece that was damaging to Anne. Her mother didn't want Anne to see her in a negative sexual light; and of course no mother would want her daughter to experience the emotional strife involved with infidelity or to face the decision to have an abortion or not. But in the end it was how Anne's mother handled her sexual discord that hurt Anne. She didn't want her daughter to be ashamed of *her*, but she went about achieving it in a way that shamed her *daughter*. Anne's mother used her own sexual dread to punish Anne for "crimes" she hadn't committed, before she had even had any sexual experiences to be ashamed of. This is the downside of what we, as mothers, believe to be our own good intentions toward our daughters: in an effort to protect them we often fail to give them the respect or the room to live their own lives.

We send our daughters negative messages about their sexuality and ours, not only through what we say but also through silent omission. In doing this, we teach our girls to hide their vibrancy and natural curiosity, and we lead them away from learning how to follow their own instincts. Even though they need to individuate from us in order to become adults, there's a difference between healthy individuation and a maternally imposed distance around the topic of all things sexual. They will need the model of intimacy in our relationship with them to help them develop the skills necessary to weather any turbulence they'll encounter in sexually intimate relationships, tools like: honest communication, discussion, entitlement to their erotic life, and the ability to weigh decisions and consequences as they see fit. As mothers we need to remember that sexuality isn't just about the body. It is very much about the mind, which takes counsel from the heart. If we taint her connection to her sexuality we're also tainting the rest of her because her feelings and thoughts are inextricably intertwined with who she is as a sexual creature—just like they are in us.

We need to accept the responsibility of teaching our daughters about sexuality throughout their lives. When our girls are little many of us sidestep the issue in ways that include such things as neglecting to teach them the correct names of their genitalia, telling ourselves they're too young to need to know. This is a discomfort that mothers have been passing on for generations, from a time when women lived with far less freedom and information than we now have. We don't teach our daughters today because we were never taught by our mothers, so it feels odd and inappropriate to us. But when we look at it from a more modern perspective, we can see that *not* teaching them is what's odd. The clearest evidence of this is that we begin preparing our girls for absolutely everything else from an early age exactly *because* our fantasies of them are fixed on the future. When they play with dolls we imagine them as mothers, and when their teddy bear's well-worn arm falls off and they tape it back on, we imagine them as doctors. We don't scoff at signing our daughters up for Little League because their bones and musculature haven't fully developed, and we don't warn them not to make friends with other children because they're too young to appreciate the sophisticated workings of interpersonal life. Even at the earliest, we imagine who they might be when they grow up and set about helping them become their best selves. We're brimming with anticipation for our daughters' development and have no problem whatsoever seeing that each experience they have will contribute to who they'll become. It comes to us effortlessly. All except for sexuality, that is. It's as if all of those nonsexual experiences live in the Land of Hope, and sexuality in the Land of Dread. For many of us, when we see even a hint of sexual curiosity in our daughters our minds freeze because we haven't learned how to handle it. In all of these ways we in effect say to our daughters, "We want you to develop into the happiest adult you can be, so go out and experience the full vibrancy of all of the parts of your life. Just not your sexuality."

It's ironic then that we begin our relationships with our infant daughters blanketed in a sensual bond. We express our love through offering and receiving physical sensations, and we see this as a celebration of life and connectedness. We nuzzle the down of their hair, breath in their baby scent, and wonder at the softness of their skin. They in turn melt into our arms, wrap all their tiny fingers around one of ours, and love for us to rock them to sleep.

Then, somewhere along the line, we forsake our reverence for this kind of human connection of the body and the senses. As they get older we move away from appreciating the importance of that innocent sensuality and its lifelong ability to convey feeling without words. We begin replacing sensuality's worth with our fears about a more sexualized version of sensual connection. And we do this even though we as grown women long for those moments when we ourselves can be immersed in those feelings. From the innocent sensual tie to our daughters to the adult sexualized sensuality we crave with our lovers, on some level we understand the value of sensuality throughout the life cycle. But for many mothers the idea of our daughters having sex is hard to accept. So rather than sharing our appreciation of sensuality and sexuality with them, over time and in age-appropriate ways, we let our yearning for their sexual safety, or our denial that they will ever have sex, stand in the way of our conveying the importance of those qualities. But it is possible to adopt a more honest view of the sexuality of mothers and daughters, in which we can support our daughters' safety while simultaneously respecting each other's sexual nature.

HOW I CAME TO WRITE THIS BOOK: THE WOMEN'S REALITIES STUDY

I wanted to find a way to give women a chance to release the shame they feel when they think no one else is feeling what they're feeling. I've learned through my career that there's an undeniable pattern of how shame and fear of being alone in one's experience interrupts the flow of healthy development. Sometimes in a given week in my practice I'll hear several women report the same problem or dilemma. For example, when it comes to sexuality, one woman will worry that she is the only one struggling with a loss of sexual attraction for her partner, another that she is the only single woman who desperately yearns to be in a couple, another that she is the only one to feel what she feels about a terminated pregnancy, and still another who feels alone in avoiding sex since having endured a rape. They'll each be embarrassed because they believe that this is happening to them alone, when in actuality they have a huge community of others silently going through similar struggles. When I assure them of this, it normalizes their experience, and the sense of belonging it creates relieves them. In spite of how talkative women are about many aspects of their lives, they don't tend to share things over which they feel shame. Therefore, because they aren't talking about them with each other, they don't know other women are going through the very same things they are; and I thought to myself, "Why should only therapists and priests be privy to this information, when it could be so healing for others?" I wanted women to be able to reach out and soothe each other without having to risk anything, so I decided to set about trying to put together an anthology of anonymously collected narratives on every single major theme of being female that I could think of so women could use it in the privacy of their own homes.

My goal was to give women voice and to write the emotional/psychological companion to *Our Bodies, Ourselves*. I designed 63 open-ended questionnaires clustered under general headings, covering everything from life transitions to relationships, sexuality, mothering, mental health, careers, violence against women, appearance, and so on, and put them on a website I had created for them at womensrealities.com; and in August 2005 the Women's Realities Study was launched.[3]

I wanted the women participating in the study to feel like they were in a therapy session and could talk about anything they wanted in any way they felt comfortable. My objective was to give them as much control as possible. Women of any age could answer as many or as few questionnaires as they liked, and write as much or as little they chose. I tried to make all of the questionnaires neutral in terms of sexual orientation, for example, using the word partner rather than boyfriend or husband to be as inclusive as possible. And I included a space in which participants could ask and answer questions about any topic that I'd neglected to cover. In reading the study's mission statement and in completing the questionnaires, women understood that the purpose of the study was to allow them not only to express themselves but to offer their experiences to reach out and help other women.

To begin disseminating the questionnaire, I sent out an email blast to all of the women in my world and asked them to forward it to their mothers, sisters, grandmothers—any woman they knew who might be interested. And off it went. As the study went on, I also made efforts to reach a broader, varied pool of respondents to make it as culturally balanced as I could. Most studies are designed to measure specific data and are often conducted by a team of researchers, and many are funded by organizations with an interest in proving a particular hypothesis. I designed, conducted, and funded the study and analyzed the responses myself, giving each woman's voice my eager attention. But because the women in the study wrote only about what they wanted to express and share, they are ultimately the ones who determined what it would be about. As a qualitative study, Women's Realities is unprecedented because it's the first and only one in which all of the content was self-selected by each respondent.

The 450 respondents who participated included African American, Asian American, Caucasian, Hispanic American, and Native American women; college graduates, many with advanced degrees, as well as women whose education concluded with high school; stay-at-home moms and women without children (some by choice, some not by choice); and ranged from straight to gay to bisexual single and partnered women. They reflected a gamut of professions: doctors, lawyers, Roller Derby queens, nurses, teachers, writers, artists, waitresses, computer scientists, therapists, professors, economists, assistants, mechanics, and more. The study gathered almost 1,300 questionnaires by women ranging in age from 18 to 105, hailing from 36 of the United States and countries as far flung as China and Israel.

Unfortunately, publishing first-edition reference books has fallen out of favor given the popularity of referencing online, so writing an anthology on the entire study as I had hoped to do was no longer a possibility. Book editors recommended instead that I narrow the scope of my results and publish it that way. So I let the Women's Realities respondents do this. They selected the subject of this book because it's an analysis of the three most highly trafficked questionnaires and how they're interconnected. The subjects most women wanted to talk about were: menstruation, women's relationships with their mothers, and, quite surprisingly, masturbation. In compiling the results and writing this book, I found that it was impossible for me to contemplate the responses to the three most popular questionnaires without the voices of the women from the other 60 informing their meaning. What one woman would write in the masturbation questionnaire would be echoed by another woman in the relationship with adult girlfriends questionnaire, for example, and the themes emerging from all of the women together took on more and more psychological and sociological weight.

The result, *Modern Mothering*, is the first book to address the psychological and emotional elements of the sexuality of *both* mothers and daughters. It offers mothers outward and inward prescriptions for change, because it's intended to encourage mothers to be introspective and reflect on our own sexuality while learning how to give our daughters the ability to live more comfortably with theirs. And it will show mothers how this can be done without intruding on our daughters' privacy or forsaking our own. This isn't about breaking down the door. It's about leaving it open.

WHAT WE HAVE TO GAIN

Our narratives, like the narratives in this book, are our own subjective stories of who we are and how we believe we got there. Each of them is unique to us, but we all have them. They modulate over and over throughout our lifetimes each time we realize something about ourselves that we hadn't thought about before and reconsider our experiences anew. It's in the fluidity of our narratives that hope is located, because even if our narrative has been bleak, it's still always able to flow in a new direction and is therefore able to change.

Mixing our own narratives with the realities of other women's lives as they're offered here can help us come together to break a cycle of dysfunction we've inherited simply by having been born female. I'll contextualize what women wanted to share with each other by exploring and weaving together the emotional and psychological import of their narratives—how they expose why we feel what we feel, and how that in turn influences why we do what we do.

Despite how far we've come in breaking the glass ceiling in many areas of our lives, we still spend vast amounts of energy teaching our daughters to focus on weight, dieting, physical imperfection, and the dangers associated with sex. Conversely, we spend little energy helping our girls grow into women who feel comfortable with their bodies and sexuality. We give them far too much of what they don't need and not nearly enough of what they do, setting our daughters up to move through their lives in an unhealthy haze that undermines their confidence, colors how they see themselves in every aspect of their lives, and can lead to depression, anxiety, eating disorders, substance abuse, self-mutilation, and unhealthy sexual relationships.

As a therapist and mother, I know today's mothers have the opportunity to provide more encompassing mothering than we probably received ourselves. My mission isn't to blame mothers; it's to expand our definition of mothering to include our blessing of our daughters' sexuality. This will lead to healthier daughters, and it will allow mothers to find new freedoms in how they see themselves as women and parents. In this grassroots way, mothers and daughters will have a hand in changing our culture.

When we see that our daughters are on the same sexual continuum as we are, we can more naturally teach them about female sexuality. Understanding this connection will embolden us as mothers to do things differently than our own mothers did. But before we can teach our daughters about body integrity, the complexity of sexuality, and the value of eroticism, we have to appreciate it in ourselves. We cannot expect them to be comfortable in their bodies or their sexual expression if we're not even comfortable *talking* about these things with them. In the following chapters we can reflect on how our own mothers' awkwardness or silence has directly impacted our ability to feel entitled to be sexually engaged; and then we will be able to ask ourselves if we want to impact our daughters in the same way.

In connecting to the psychological context and real-life anecdotes here, women will feel guided in raising daughters with healthier attitudes toward their bodies and their sexuality. We'll better understand how our own mothers may have unconsciously worked against us and how we may be unconsciously working against our daughters and what we can do to change that. We can learn clear and simple ways to reframe the way we think about female rites of passage—and replace the ignorance and shame that we've historically attached to these cornerstones with vitality and confidence.

Today, more than ever, our daughters need our guidance to grow into healthy and whole young women. According to the most recent UNICEF study, we have the highest teenage birthrate of any developed country and are tied with Hungary for the most abortions[4]; eating disorders and self-mutilating behaviors are on the rise; anxiety and depression abound.

And we're just beginning to see how technology has jumped into the ring of sexuality with the advent of sexting and cyber-bullying. There's much talk about how fathers need to step up as positive role models for their sons. It's time to talk about how we mothers can do the same for our daughters.

The findings from my research on the importance of mothers educating their daughters on sexual health, vitality, and body image concurs with the findings of other highly respected organizations, professionals, and authors. These include the American Academy of Child and Adolescent Psychiatry[5]; the American Academy of Pediatrics[6]; Columbia University, Cornell University, and UCLA[7]; the Wellesley College Centers for Research on Women[8]; Harvard University's Gender Studies program; feminist Naomi Wolf[9]; and public health and sex education experts.[10]

After more than two decades of practice, I know full well it's what we learn in the homes we grow up in that most strongly determines the development of our personalities and our perspectives. And as mothers we need to understand that it's there, in those seemingly mundane inter-actions with our daughters while we're getting dressed, or taking plates down from the cupboard, that their views of themselves and the world are shaped. We need to be mindful that our influence on our daughters comes not only from the things we say directly to them, but also from conversations or remarks our daughters overhear, like "I was good today. I skipped lunch." In addition, things such as the loud absence of a maternal voice in the years surrounding a daughter's first period can likewise have lasting effects. One of these comments or omissions on their own would likely be forgettable, but when these influences are accumulated over a lifetime and echoed in the world around us they have a lasting impact. But if mothers change the message and strengthen themselves to be role models valued for their minds, hearts, and bodies—no matter the shape or size—as women who have the freedom to fully embrace their sexuality, then daughters will feel more grounded, confident, and connected, making them less susceptible to suffering and damaging behaviors as well as more inclined to reenact positive behaviors with their own daughters when the time comes. In 2009, during a series of shows on female sexuality, *Oprah* brought to millions of viewers Jordan, a little 10-year-old girl who must surely be the most delightful child ever to appear on television. In her own words, she presented the most poignant and concise message about mother-daughter sexuality. She'd been asking her mother twice a week for the past eight months to please teach her about sex, and her wonderful yet anxious mother was scared to death she'd say the wrong thing. During the episode Jordan was asked, "Do you have any ideas about what sex is?" And she replied, "It's not like I have the confidence to think about that, but I want *my mom* to have the confidence to talk to me about it."[11]

Recent decades have brought a sharp rise in interest in expanding women's sexual understanding of themselves, from psychological and medical research to television shows devoted exclusively to the topic. Uniting women and girls in their sexual confidence is the next historical phase in understanding and embracing female sexuality, and it is important on so many levels. Women are eager for more information about ourselves, and exploring the organic flow of this information from mother to daughter is at the heart of this endeavor. Knowing each other at a more intimate level will let us grow further into our own sexual comfort as women. It can give our daughters the gift of helping them skip the guilt, shame, and ignorance that has been inextricably linked to female sexuality. And it will strengthen our gender by showing us how to support ourselves and our daughters by replacing our ingrained habits of sabotaging each other with lessons on how to ground our sexuality in a sense of *home*, mother to daughter.

It's never too late for mothers and daughters to learn from each other and to appreciate what we value. For my study, I had the privilege of interviewing in person a woman who was 105 years old. Even though this isn't a story directly about her mother, I'm sharing it because it shows us how profoundly important our sexuality is over our lifetimes. When I went to California to meet this outstanding woman, who walked out to greet me in an elegant dress and had a better short-and long-term memory than I've ever had, she was introduced to me by one of her relatives as "Gammy."

Together she and I went over the list of questionnaire subjects she could choose from. When I asked her which ones she wanted our interview to cover, she gave me a wry sidelong glance, and with a flick of her head, she said, "Let's do marriage."

As we worked our way through the questions, she disclosed that just as World War II was looming her husband began an affair, and that, in a house full of children, she and her husband lived as total strangers for two years. She described this period of living the lie of a happy marriage as the worst time of her life, and while she had told no one of her husband's affair, she said, "I had one very good old friend who knew that my husband was not any longer in love with me...." Then she looked me directly in the eye and said, "I'd have *died* without her," and she began to cry in remembering this act of friendship. When I asked her to describe the finest moment of her marriage she said, "The night he took me upstairs, and we had our first sex in two years!" I asked her what it meant to her. "Everything" was her answer. She then went on to confide that prior to that renewing evening, she, in an act of vengeance, had begun her own brief affair, and that I was the only person she had ever told.

"Gammy" made me look beyond what society tells us we'll find in the elderly: an antiseptic little old lady with white cotton-candy hair. She made sure I saw who she was: a woman in full. At 105, this was what *she* wanted to talk about.

* * *

TWO NOTES ABOUT THIS BOOK

1. All clinical case content from my practice has been disguised to protect anonymity; pseudonyms have been used, and certain identifying information changed in the service of upholding privacy. For the two older women I interviewed in person for the Women's Realities Study ("Gammy" and Ruth) I have used pseudonyms, but all other study respondents have complete anonymity, and their narratives have been kept in their own words.

2. Almost everything in this book is an examination of women's own responsibility to our daughters and ourselves; that focus didn't include an examination of the responsibility men need to take to help move us toward a fair society. Venturing into that field was beyond the scope of this book. My aim is to highlight what we as women can change in ourselves, not to blame the victim or to excuse men but to actualize in ourselves powers we already have at our disposal. While both parents and culture shape how girls come to live in their sexuality, this book is based on my study of women. It is not meant to shortchange the influence of fathers, other primary caretakers, or culture.

Chapter One

How Our Mothers Influence Us

*T*his book's Introduction explained the importance of letting our daughters see us as full sexual beings, but, to date, sexuality hasn't been a comfortable part of the mother-daughter bond. We seek nurturing and understanding from our mothers. We lavish affection and support on our daughters. Knowing our mothers as real flesh-and-blood women with thwarted loves, desires, and disappointments can be more complicated.

Many of us don't want to think about our mothers having sex because doing so comes with a little mental movie we'd rather not see. One of my friends playfully refers to this phenomenon as The Ick Factor. Our resistance to contemplating such sexual images is understandable because the mother-daughter relationship isn't a sexualized one, so our thoughts don't easily wander there. This also explains why it works both ways, and we mothers can find it just as uncomfortable to envision our daughters having sex. But even if we're uncomfortable imagining these private acts, we have to be careful not to throw the baby out with the bathwater, because disregarding the importance of our sexuality is another matter entirely. A failure to honor in each other the vital role that sexuality plays over our lifetimes—in how we feel alive and in how we love—greatly inhibits our ability to have what mothers and daughters would both ultimately wish for each other: a life well lived.

So how do we honor sexuality without feeling like we're crossing boundaries we shouldn't be? Over the past few years I've lectured on the results of my study to groups of women. When I begin talking about female sexuality, and how it's passed on from mother to daughter, a light electrical current of something approaching panic usually runs through the audience and a woman will raise her hand and ask, "Are you advocating that we share the specifics of our sex lives with our daughters?" The answer is more complex than yes or no. Of course, sharing too much of the sexual detail of our lives would be inappropriate for our daughters. What I advocate is giving our daughters, slowly and in small doses, the informational and emotional support that will foster the same sense of well-being in their sexuality that we'd want for them in any other area of their lives. I'm advocating an openness that makes it clear to our daughters that teaching them about their sexuality is far from being something to fear, it is a *privilege* of mothering. As our daughters learn that they can trust us to be supportive and straightforward with them about sexuality, they'll gradually internalize this confidence and transform it into a deepening ability to understand and trust themselves. And this is exactly what they'll need to make sexually healthy choices and to experience the vibrancy of erotic love without shame.

Sadly, we often have the opposite effect on our daughters. We can be so afraid of venturing into anything sexual that we retreat too far, leaving our daughters out in the cold—confused and feeling unsupported. One woman in my study who wanted to be closer to her mother, who she wished had taught her about her sexuality, had so little faith in her mother that she'd have settled for any family member. *I wish a family member had explained it—although I have yet to have sex explained to me by anyone and I'm 32 years old.* Instead of being supported she was left alone. While she obviously would have done some learning on her own and on the fly, like many women, no one took the time to explain sex to her as she was growing into her sexuality over time, within the intimacy of familial relationships. Now, at 32, it would probably feel too humiliating for her to ask for input even from those closest to her. Of course she can educate herself through reading, but that won't necessarily feel less emotionally empty, and it certainly won't provide the warm bond she wanted with her mother.

If our goal is to support our daughters in the quest of a life well lived, we have to pay attention to the messages we give them along the way. Which messages help a daughter feel grounded and confident, and which introduce self-consciousness and shame? As I hope to show in the following pages, mothers still experience discomfort in educating their daughters about menstruation. If our own discomfort gets in the way of that, imagine the unspoken, often unconscious, fear of teaching them about their sexuality—which would by extension also be teaching them about ours. How can we expect our daughters to hold their own in the bafflingly complex world of sexual relationships, and unrealistic images of sexuality in the media or on the internet, when they sense our own impairments to being comfortable in discussing our own sexuality and making it part of the mother-daughter relationship?

Some mothers can try to hide the topic altogether in the belief that they are protecting their daughters by postponing "the conversation." I'll broach it when they're ten, they say. Then they promise themselves to get it to by the twelfth birthday. By the next promised benchmark, they realize their daughters have already been educated or miseducated by the internet, media and their peers amid the turbulence and confusion of the teenage years.

The truth is, we're teaching them about sexuality whether we think we are or not. It's just a matter of *what* we're teaching. Our daughters observe and weigh our every move, conversation, silence, gesture, and relationship. One adult daughter reflects on this reality. She says that the most complex facet of her relationship with her mother is *her lack of living in her sexuality, and her resentment of men, which drives me up the wall. It compromised my ability to make good decisions and to have confidence in relationships with men. I have had to learn just about everything by trial and error—what a mess.*

It's true that daughters have to learn from their own experiences, but they're still always influenced by their mothers' views and behavior. Examining our impact on them from the time they're little will help us focus our efforts on trying to affect them in ways that enhance their growth rather than detract from it. It will be harder for our daughters if we only start seeing them as sexual once they're adults. We need to be there with them from the beginning of the journey as they start to have questions about body parts and where babies come from, and as they need help understanding their desires. And to better understand how crucial that journey is, we need to see the value in psychological and sexual development—how our daughters' sense of self will develop as our baby girls, day by day, grow into the women they will be.

WOMEN AND PERSONALITY DEVELOPMENT THEORY

How we become who we are is a process that begins at birth, or some would argue, in utero. In psychology this is known as the development of a personality, and it's been the foundational theory of the human mind ever since Sigmund Freud opened it for the Western world around the turn of the twentieth century.

The pertinence of studying personality development for therapists is that it helps us understand what leads to a more or less healthy personality, and what leads to one that suffers to the extent that healthy functioning is interrupted. Once we understand what caused a person's emotional hardship and how they dealt with it, we can have a better sense of how to help that individual. Centuries of clinical and medical practice have taught us that our minds and our bodies are interconnected and that personality development and sexual development can't be separated from each other. When people try to divorce the two, it's often at a great emotional cost.

And yet we live in a society where women are taught to neglect half of who we are—half of our very existence. In case studies from Harvard

Medical School, psychologists have noted that trying to make female sexuality conform to male sexuality has led to a misunderstanding of women and kept us from seeing the unique nature of female sexuality.[1] And this is where mothers can use developmental theory the same way therapists do. If we understand the ways we can have a negative impact on our daughters' growth—their personality development and their sexual development—we'll be in a far better position to raise happy, healthy girls who become happy, healthy women.

Here's a brief history of how the understanding of female sexuality has progressed. Although Freud began his career listening to women's reports of inappropriate "seduction" by men, he abandoned his seduction theory and instead mapped the conscious, preconscious, and unconscious mind and delineated the psychic structure of the ego, superego, and id. As a thinker of the Victorian period, his stages of psychosexual development—oral, anal, phallic, and Oedipal—were designed around the centrality of male sexuality, mainly, the assumption that girls envied boys their penises. However, even though this focus on male sexuality was accepted, and both parents were acknowledged as affecting their children's psyches, since women have traditionally been the ones in charge of child rearing, the power of the mother-child bond has always held the focus of theorists' attention. As time went on, other psychoanalysts and doctors stretched Freud's ideas as the science advanced, but updating notions of female sexuality didn't make much progress, due to the old-guard resistance encountered whenever someone attempted it. Since the second wave of feminism, though, more of the female experience has been studied, with later writers bringing in gender theory to balance out the early male-heavy perspectives. Now, in the third wave of feminism, the movement to construct a fuller appreciation of women continues to build steam. Adding to our growing understanding of how female sexuality differs from that of males, the field of sexology is garnering more respect than ever. Female psychologists are conducting sexual research on women, and in addition to their measurement of psychological data, they're enlivening it with biological and neuroscientific data as well.[2]

This convergence of psychology and gender theory, influenced by neuropsychology, feminism, and sexual research, has created a space where the psychology of both male and female sexuality can be understood and valued. We're entering an exciting era in which these studies will inform our understanding of how girls become women and a mother's role in that unfolding. The next frontier—*female sexuality from women's own perspective as they experience it*—is ours for the creating. This book is an offering to that end, an exploration of the undeniable link in the personality and sexual development of both mother and daughter.

HOW A MOTHER'S INFLUENCE BEGINS

We're all a product of the balance between nature and nurture—the interplay of raw material we're born with and how it's either cared for or compromised by our parents. The forces that shape female sexuality come from all directions: family, culture, social environment, schools, political and religious beliefs, the internet, the media, physical and mental health, the presence or absence of trauma...the possibilities for what influences us are vast. Each of them carries great weight, but my focus is the relationship between mother and daughter and its impact on sexual development. As mothers are typically the ones who do the lion's share of caretaking, even in households with working mothers, their impact on daughters is powerful—their common gender makes this impact complex and formative. Jessica Benjamin, of New York University, finds in her work and research that girls assume their gender identity in the first two years of life by identifying with their mothers.[3] We are our daughters' model of what it means to be female from the time they're born. No matter whether they embrace elements of us or reject them, as mothers, our behaviors and perspectives are forces to be reckoned with.

This is true about many aspects of our lives, not just in sexual development. Take, for instance, shopping. If your mother loves to shop for herself and you've seen it bring her pleasure while you were growing up, you probably won't feel guilty shopping for yourself. That new book or those new shoes will feel like a small celebration you're welcome to enjoy. On the other hand, if your mother felt guilty whenever she shopped for herself and you saw it distress her—maybe through fretting beforehand, hiding new purchases, or lamenting how much money she'd spent—you'll likely grow into a woman who finds it hard to pamper herself in this way. Even if you work to overcome it, its imprint will linger on your psyche.

The more things we observe about our mothers, the more we develop an understanding of them as women, including their sexuality. And since our understanding of our mothers as women informs our understanding of ourselves, its meaning is doubled in strength, and its influence on us becomes that much more powerful. Much of this understanding of women and sexuality is fully in our conscious awareness, but some of it is experienced on a preconscious or unconscious level, and things that are preconscious or unconscious are sort of like the air we breathe; we can't see it, but its presence is constant. To capture the phenomenon of inherited traits, I offer a representative sample of what women in my Women's Realities Study reported in response to the question: "What personality trait did you inherit from your mother that you love or respect?" Many of the statements quoted here reveal how, over time, inherited traits become a part of our daughters and inform their futures.

Responsibility. My mother would make us go to school every day. We always had perfect attendance. Even when I didn't want to go she motivated me to keep my commitments. I went to school with chicken pox when I was 11 because she was determined to teach us responsibility. She felt bad when she realized it was the chicken pox, but it is still a story that is told repeatedly.

* * *

Independence. She was in business for herself from when I was preschool age, and I eventually became an entrepreneur myself. I am sure I got that gene from her.

* * *

I am a caring person to strangers. I became a nurse. Perhaps I became a nurse because I thought then people would love me too, like strangers loved my mother. Of course, it did not work out that way, but I did enjoy my profession and was good at it.

* * *

I too am tenacious. We are both fighters.

* * *

I am warm like my mother. She had a welcoming and warm home… everyone loved being there… she knew how to nurture people.

* * *

Wit and kindness… and love of people and conversation. It's part of me.

Responses to the question "What personality trait of your mother's do you have that you hate or disrespect?" included:

Critical of others.

* * *

Vanity, self-loathing.

* * *

Letting people walk over us. She doesn't say no and takes shit from everyone. Especially men.

* * *

Making people feel guilty.

* * *

There are several: Knowing something is hurtful or petty and saying it anyway; excessive, unproductive worrying; self-criticism; self-sabotage;

self-loathing. I tune into a lot of negative things, like my mom, and I believe I would be more focused, more ambitious, and more accomplished if I could get out from under these behavior patterns.

* * *

I can say cutting things to my daughters that I know she said to me.

Daughters begin absorbing our patterns of interaction earlier than many of us think. It wasn't too long ago that our culture believed babies were little bundles largely incapable of anything. The groundbreaking infant researcher Daniel Stern found that actually the "first two months of life the infant is actively forming a sense of an emergent self...that will remain active for the rest of life." Stern has a beautiful phrase for this. He calls it "coming into being."[4] He found that babies are predesigned to be capable of much more than was previously thought. Three-day-old infants can discern the smell of their own mother's milk from that of other mothers'; newborns can be trained to suck to get something to happen, like getting a slide carousel to click through pictures; and blindfolded three-week-old infants can visually recognize whether the nipple they just sucked was smooth or nubby. Each of these amazing discoveries shows that babies have the ability to "know" things. And Stern's findings were just the beginning. In the most current infant research, Alison Gopnik, psychology professor at the University of California at Berkeley, shows in her book *The Philosophical Baby* that the more we study babies the more astoundingly sophisticated they reveal themselves to be. Among their complex capacities, for example, are the ability to detect statistical probability and a young but innate understanding of empathy.[5]

Knowing that even newborns are sophisticated enough to observe, measure, and take in what gradually becomes their experienced knowledge base can help us appreciate how, from birth, our mothers come to have an unparalleled role in our womanhood. We might not become exact replicas of our mothers, but we do all internalize aspects of them that stay with us forever. This is not to say that mothers bear sole responsibility for making or breaking their daughters' lives, only that the intensity of a mother's mark on her daughter is irrefutable. As we consider our impact on our daughters' sexual development we'll see that our efforts to help them flourish in this area could be drastically improved.

As the first step in understanding ourselves as sexual women and how we pass on those values to our daughters, we need to examine how our views on sexuality were molded by what our own mothers did or didn't say, and did or didn't reveal. If we want to be there for our daughters and teach them about their bodies, sexuality, and desire, we need to have an understanding of our own erotic life and its highly personal meaning to us. And we need to consider not just where we are now, but how we got there from girlhood, and what we hope for ourselves in the future

What follows is a list of questions to get mothers thinking. At first glance some of these questions might appear simplistic, but bear with me because they're actually quite thought provoking. Think about the question "How old are you?" Seems simple enough. But whenever someone asks me that, after I give my age it sets off a chain reaction of synapse sparks. What does being 49 mean to me? What's changed since 39, 29, 19, and 9? Am I where I want to be? How have I come through for myself, and how have I let myself down? How well have I loved? How do I feel about where my relationships are? What were my fantasies of what my life would be like at 49, and what's the reality? How's my health, my sexuality, what changes have I seen in my body and my face? What have I accomplished? What dreams have died, what dreams have come true, and what dreams are still floating out there?

The questions have been clustered into three groups representing the continuum of sexuality that comes from our mothers, goes through us, and then makes its way onto our daughters.[6] Our inner selves were shaped by our mothers, and now that we're in a maternal role, we're in a position to shape our daughters' inner experience.

I hope that by thinking about these questions, you give yourself a chance to look at your sexuality through a new lens and deepen your understanding of how your mother's sexuality links to yours, which in turn, links to your daughter's.

OUR MOTHERS

Questions a Mother Can Ask Herself as She Considers Her Mother's Sexuality

- ☐ Do I know what my mother's sexual existence is/was like? How do I know this?
- ☐ Do I want to have a sense of what my mother's sexual sense of herself is/was? Why or why not? What would it mean to me?
- ☐ Do I feel my mother values/valued her sexuality? How did I come to feel that?
- ☐ Do I feel my mother values/valued my sexuality? How was that value or lack of value communicated to me?
- ☐ How do I wish my mother had seen my sexuality when I was going through adolescence?
- ☐ What would it mean to me if my mother had had many sexual partners over her lifetime?
- ☐ Do I hope that at some point in my mother's life she felt sexually swept away? Why or why not? What would it mean to me, and what would it say about her?
- ☐ What do I hope she experiences/experienced in her sexuality and desire throughout her life? Why is that what I would wish for her?
- ☐ What part of me wants to be sexually like her, and what part of me wants to be different, and why?

OURSELVES

Questions a Mother Can Ask Herself as She Considers Her Own Sexuality

- ☐ When I was a girl, did I ever feel confused, frightened, alone, naughty, or dirty with regard to my sexuality? Am I positioning my daughter to feel any of those things?
- ☐ How did my mother disappoint me in helping me learn about my sexuality?
- ☐ How did my mother come through for me in helping me learn about my sexuality?
- ☐ Have I really allowed myself the right to my own erotic desires? What memories reveal this?

- ☐ Do I have memories of being disconnected from my body, or being unable to get turned on because I was focusing more on what my partner was feeling? If so, what feeling or worry caused the disconnection?

- ☐ How often do I undermine my own arousal by getting preoccupied with what I see as my physical flaws? Have I ever let my focus on my perceived flaws get in the way of hearing how my partner desires me?

- ☐ When I think of other women who are turned on in movies I see or books I read, do I ever think, "I wish I were like that"? What's the quality I see in them that I want in myself?

- ☐ What was the best sex of my life, when I felt totally consumed by my own fire, and what did I—*not my partner*—do to participate in having it feel that way?

- ☐ Looking back, what erotic freedoms did I deny myself, and why?

- ☐ If I could live out the fantasy of being my best and happiest sexual self, how would it be different than what I allow myself in reality?

- ☐ How do I want my sexual sense of myself to expand by allowing myself all that I want for my *daughter*?

OUR DAUGHTERS

Questions a Mother Can Ask Herself as She Considers Her Daughter's Sexuality

- ☐ How might my daughter interpret my silence or reluctance to talk to her about her body and her sexuality?

- ☐ Will she think I believe it's wrong to talk about her sexuality? Will she think I believe it's abnormal? Perverted? Not worth the time?

- ☐ Have I taught her the names and functions of her genitals and reproductive system? If not, what stopped me?

- ☐ Have I taken the lead in talking to her so the onus isn't always on her to ask questions?

- ☐ If my young daughter has a question about her sexuality, do I want her to think I don't want her to come to me? How do I expect her to know this?

- ☐ Do I want her to feel she can come to me throughout her life with sexual questions if she has them? How have I conveyed this to her?

- ☐ What have I thought about saying to her but chickened out on? What fear made me chicken out?

- ☐ What percentage of what I've taught her has focused on the dangers of sex and what percentage has been on the lusciousness of it?

- ☐ Do I indirectly want her to have unfulfilling sex?

- ☐ Do I want her to be able to feel alive and connected not only to her lovers but to herself when she acts on her desire? How have I actively supported this grounding in herself?

- ☐ Do I want her adult life to include the vibrancy of sexuality and sensuality? What have I actively said and done to help that happen?

- [ ] Do I want her to be able to know and ask for what arouses her? How do I expect her to come by that confidence?

- [ ] Have I really conveyed to her that I want her happiness to include feeling entitled to her erotic life?

- [ ] Do I critique her body or my own in front of her? How do I imagine this will affect her confidence and how she expresses herself with her body in and out of bed?

A REAL-LIFE EXAMPLE OF HOW IT WORKS

For a real-life example, I return one last time to the *Oprah* series on female sexuality that I referred to in the Introduction. I want to do this before I go into the specifics of my own findings because it will help mothers see that the issues expressed in my study and practice are replicated in our culture at large, and have already been witnessed by millions of women. So, to bookend the daughter's perspective offered earlier, here is a story from a mother's standpoint. In one of the episodes a guest panelist, the comedian and actress Ali Wentworth, offered up the perfect everywoman example of a point at which our inherited views of sexuality collide with our daughters' future understanding. Winfrey and Wentworth were commenting on a prior show in which the sex therapist Dr. Laura Berman strongly advocated that mothers speak more openly with their daughters about sexuality. In particular, Berman spoke about the benefits of teaching our daughters about masturbation so that they could have a sense of ownership over their sexual response cycle. Many of the women in the audience literally stammered with discomfort at the thought of how to take in this professional recommendation. Some women couldn't say the word at all, and when others did try they were so overcome that the word that actually ended up coming out was *m-m-masturbation*. It was like the sexual equivalent of saying "Voldemort."

While Winfrey was recapping the lessons Berman had doled out, Wentworth shared an incident between herself, her husband, George Stephanopoulos, and their six-year-old daughter, Elliott. Said Wentworth,

> Listen, your show was a big a-ha moment for me as a parent. My
> kids are still young, but I started to really think about what I am

going to say...Elliott...came in and caught me and George having marital, carnal, carnivorous relations...The door was closed—[but] she came in! She was like, "Daddy? What are you doing to Mommy?" And it was interesting to see our reactions. I said [in a girlish giggle], "Daddy's tickling me!" And George said [in a warm adult tone], "Honey, we're making love." But what I realized from this show is that I need to be more open and give them information. I will talk to my daughters about masturbation.7

Wentworth illustrates how we can re-envision ourselves as mothers who are less afraid of educating our daughters on sexuality: Take some new sexual information, mix it with a dose of self-reflection, and give it to our daughters and ourselves to bring on a stronger and fuller sense of self. Her story is great because it captures a situation any of us could imagine finding ourselves in and being at a complete loss for what to say. I applaud that, after the fact, Wentworth took the new information she'd gotten from the show on sexuality, combined it with her husband's alternative perception of the lovemaking scene, and used them to reevaluate her own thinking. She saw it as a pivotal moment in reassessing the importance of being more open in teaching her girls about sexuality because she'd found a new appreciation for how it would contribute to their sexual well-being as they matured. And, I would argue, it also positioned her to rethink her own entitlement to fully claim her sexuality as a mother, an aspect of themselves mothers from previous generations would have felt compelled to hide or deny. It presented her with an opportunity to consider being sexually authentic in a way her own mother most likely didn't teach her to be. Wentworth's desire to raise her girls with a growing sense of their own sexuality pulled her through to a new, more realistic and cohesive way of experiencing being a woman and a mother. We need to understand that a mother, just as a father, can, in a warm adult tone, begin to reveal herself as a sexual being to her daughter whether this occurs through our planned efforts, or as in Wentworth's case, when we are taken by surprise.

Wentworth's story is also of note because it represents the dichotomy between the liberation we've won and the tenacity with which our culture still contains our right to sexual vibrancy. Even within the bounds of the *one* way our society "approves" of female sexuality—the institution of marriage between man and woman— the lack of maternal education and cultural support we've had causes us to be arrested by awkwardness and befuddled in how to react "appropriately." No one has prepared us to see ourselves favorably as our daughters' healthy sexual role models—and by that I mean as grown women who desire and have sex. Even in heterosexual marriage, this remains a taboo for mothers.

In her international best seller *Mating in Captivity*, author Esther Perel says that the sexual invisibility of the American mother is so ingrained in our national psyche that both men and women conspire to deny maternal sexuality. She continues, "We are afraid that our adult sexuality will somehow damage our kids, that it's inappropriate or dangerous. But whom are we protecting? Children who see their primary caregivers at ease expressing their affection (discreetly, within appropriate boundaries) are more likely to embrace sexuality with the healthy combination of respect, responsibility, and curiosity it deserves. By censoring our sexuality, curbing our desires, or renouncing them altogether, we hand our inhibitions intact to the next generation."[8]

We as mothers can be good role models if we're cognizant of wanting to send messages to our daughters that support their incremental emergence into womanhood. But if we remain unaware of the importance of imparting sexual information as we feel appropriate, or are inclined to feel really uncomfortable with such information, it can harm our daughters. Let's say that from the age of one to 20 a daughter received countless conscious and unconscious messages from her mother that female sexuality is somehow too upsetting to be discussed in polite company. This is where mothers do their daughters a disservice, because all of those messages are internalized. Unless it's traumatic, one incident doesn't have the power to skew a daughter's emergent sense of her sexual self. What becomes problematic is the accumulation of negative message after negative message that string together to form a reliable pattern, because once a child takes in a pattern as reliable, they take it in as a reality. And we can't expect them to do otherwise. If a mother has proven this to be *her* reality over and over again, it is also the *girl's reality* because they're living it out together.

Things that interfere with the smooth development of our sexual selves by and large come from two means. From trauma, such as sexual abuse or rape, and, as noted, from ongoing messages, routine comments, or silences that happen over years and years. In treatment I often liken these influences to the difference between the damage created by an earthquake versus that of beach erosion. Huge obvious change can occur in our psychological landscape in an instant or almost imperceptibly, grain by grain of sand.

Stephen Mitchell of New York University explained how this pattern of repeated messages works from a clinical standpoint. He pointed out that because a mother's personality remains largely unchanged while a child is growing up, the ways she fails to relate adequately to her daughter when she was little likely remain the same throughout her daughter's development. Those patterns become so ingrained in the daughter's perspective that they influence how she approaches her life in the present.[9] This is how the past stays alive in each of us.

I know some might perceive this characterization of mothers as harsh—a failure to relate adequately—but to me it's exciting because it's hopeful. Mothers can't fix what they don't know is broken. Looking at the ways we do fail our daughters and ourselves allows us the chance to make corrections. It gives us a choice. We can protect our daughters' growing sexual integrity and our own, or we can slowly erode them. Of course we'll fail our daughters sometimes. We're human. But it should be comforting to be guided by our desire to work on contributing to patterns of health rather than erosion.

So with Mitchell's words in mind, let's explore how things could take a less-than-healthy turn for a daughter whose mother repeatedly conveys discomfort about sex. Mishandling the explanation of a lovemaking scene, like the one Ali Wentworth describes, could be just one of many other negative interchanges a daughter would witness. With the addition of each new message against sexuality, the daughter would gradually begin to believe that she has no right to an erotic existence because that is not what women, most especially women who are mothers, do. If we are always girlish about sexual matters our daughters may conclude we don't experience adult sexuality. If we always lie or dodge the truth around sex our daughters could assume we aren't comfortable with the truth, so they can't trust us to give them accurate information. If we never share any elements of our female sexuality, our daughters may think this is because female sexuality is inherently bad and needs to be hidden. If our messages have been consistent and reliable, in each of these ways, we will influence our daughters' perceptions. We can even see a smidgeon of how this could begin in the actual Wentworth account. Remember what Stern and Gopnik's babies can do, then consider what Wentworth's curious six-year-old daughter is psychologically capable of. In their story she knows something she can't classify is happening to her mother because her instincts tell her so. She knows Mommy isn't being tickled. We can assume this because she doesn't ask, "Daddy? Why are you tickling Mommy?" She asks for an explanation of what she's witnessing precisely because she doesn't have a place to put it—it doesn't fit into categories of relating that she's seen so far. Wentworth's response doesn't match her daughter's perception, so the daughter is now in a position to question her own instincts. Again, this one event is harmless, but if it were part of a pattern in which the daughter repeatedly had to adjust her own perceptions to accommodate her mother's, each time, the daughter would lose a little bit more of herself to silence or secrecy or shame. Wentworth's realization of this and her desire to think of things differently from then on, shows us how helpful reconceptualizing our inherited beliefs can be—how one small change can immeasurably benefit our daughters and free us of dusty, culturally imposed sexual restraints at the same time.

This is the juncture at which we can respond differently than our own mothers might have. If we're caught making love but say we're being tickled, our daughters are forced to suppress their own impressions in favor of their longing to believe in and learn from us. But if we realize that our daughters will benefit from straightforward information dispatched in age-appropriate ways, we will be making the choice to help our daughters uphold their perceptions and instincts. It's energizing to realize that even one new awareness of the value of sexuality can give us the chance to change what could have become a pattern of stifling ourselves and our daughters into a far healthier pattern of sexual coherence and connection.

Being more conscious of our role as women our daughters will identify with will enable us to reconsider our reflex reaction, or more accurately, our learned response, of hiding our sexuality from them. Nathalie Bartle, in her research out of Harvard University, concludes, "If anything becomes clear from the stories of mother-daughter communication, it is the importance of having an ongoing dialogue with our daughters, of piecing together the nuts and bolts for them, and broadening the context in which the facts are placed."[10] And if readers are still uncomfortable at the thought of this, it may help to know that being more open in educating our children about sex is a position advocated by the medical community as well as the psychological community. Although they acknowledge how difficult it may be for some parents, the American Academy of Child and Adolescent Psychiatry states that "talking to your children about love, intimacy, and sex is an important part of parenting."[11] And the American Academy of Pediatrics offers guidelines for teaching our children starting when they're 18 months old.[12]

We don't have to worry about making mistakes here and there. It's the ongoing nature of how we communicate that's important. And we can take our time, because creating openness is a work in progress. That's the beauty of leaving the door open: mothers and daughters can pass through it whenever they like.

We continue to come into ourselves throughout the life cycle as our experiences and the emotional registry of what we learn and know grows. As we explore how girls become women we'll see that we learn to become women in the context of other women, and for most of us the most formative female relationship we have is with our mothers. It's in knowing our mothers over time that we learn what a woman is and what being a woman means. And in terms of developing a sense of ourselves, as we're learning who our mothers are, so are we simultaneously learning who we are. We're aware of this in many regards, such as emotional similarities we share or a sense of humor that might be like our mother's, but we're not used to looking for the sense of sexuality that gets downloaded from mother to daughter. And just because we're not used to looking for it doesn't mean it's not there.

Chapter Two

Are You There, Mom? It's Me, Your Daughter

The day I received my period, my mother gave me a pad and told me never to let boys play with me "down there."

*   *   *

My mom didn't ever talk about those things....I wish my mom was more approachable or that she had addressed the topic with me. More importantly, I wish she had addressed the fact that I was an extremely late bloomer because that was very tough for me....I didn't even tell her when I got my period. She figured it out on her own and never even said anything to me.

*   *   *

I wish my mom had told me about it....I was embarrassed and worried that the kids at school would know, or that I smelled funny.

When you read statements like these, it's hard not to appreciate how far women have come in shedding the shame and discomfort that used to surround teaching our daughters about *the most fundamental feature of being female.* Or at least that would be the case if it weren't for the unfortunate truth that all of those quotes are from women in their twenties, and they're representative of almost 50 percent of the women under age 30 who responded to my menstruation questionnaire.

It's easy for us to conjure up images of mothers and daughters from the 1940s who would have gone through the onset of menstruation that way. But it's another thing to acknowledge that even today, if it weren't for Judy Blume, the internet, or the school nurse, lots of us wouldn't know anything.

Puberty is a time when a girl begins her ascent into womanhood and adult sexuality. But not only does it signal her reproductive life; it also brings complexities in her sense of herself as an individual and social being—complexities that will remain alive in her as she matures and indeed throughout her life. My interest in menstruation, which came to me through the way women in my study wrote about it, is this: How does what a girl learns or doesn't learn from her mother influence who she becomes as a woman? And more specifically, what happens to a daughter's sense of who she is in the world when her mother hasn't prepared her for menstruation and shared a sense of being alike with her in this way?

For the purposes of this chapter, when I refer to a daughter's sexuality—her sexual life and identity—I'm using it the same way I would to refer to her mental life. Her mental life represents the way she thinks and reasons; it houses her humor and her fantasy life; and through her communication of it she'll reveal its unique contents to whomever she chooses. Her sexuality, on the other hand, represents her sense of herself in her physical body. It houses her desires and what she deems private; it's the ethereal and corporal domain of her gender; and as she matures, through her sharing of it, she'll reveal the most intimate parts of her emotional life to whomever she chooses.

As our daughters go through puberty and adolescence their sexual sense of self begins a process of coalescing into an adult identity, and it will all be played out in their social world. In the beginning they'll be wondering how to cover up, or to show off, their new breast buds, and getting used to the disconcerting appearance of pubic and underarm hair. They'll be concerned about how quickly menstrual blood will flow, what it will feel like, and who will know when they have their period. They'll be stressed about whether to hide pads and tampons in their socks or in their lockers, and embarrassed to be excused from class to use the bathroom. You'll pick them up from school one day and they'll be bursting with some grown-up pride, and the next they'll dissolve in tears for no apparent reason, and this will really irritate them because they miss the happy-go-lucky days, pre-hormone takeover. As time goes on, belonging and ostracizing will become pronounced forces in their social lives, and many days will feel like a tightrope walk between the two. They'll be wondering what to make of the new sensations physical arousal causes, and processing their attraction to boys or girls, which will soon become complicated by actual sexual experimenting, in all its fear and swoon.

They'll experience touching and being touched, and the ensuing confusion and thrill. And on the home front they'll practice having total autonomy from the complete and utter embarrassment of us even as they crave snuggling when no one in their peer group is within a certain radius.

For years our daughters will live in a netherland between girlhood and womanhood, and as is the nature of transition, making the move will involve a sense of being somewhat lost as they leave something familiar for something new. Mothers can be loving guides during this time, but according to the results of the Women's Realities Study mentioned earlier, we often fall short of giving our daughters what they need, with menstruation being the lightning rod for their disappointment in us.

Things that aren't openly discussed are often intimately acquainted with shame, and as we can see from the opening quotes in this chapter, menstruation is one of those things. In *Reviving Ophelia*, Mary Pipher succinctly describes the anatomical and interpersonal components of girls' maturation. "Puberty is defined as a biological process while adolescence is defined as the social and personal experience of that process."[1] If what happens to us biologically is attached to social and personal shame, it doesn't bode well for a female's confidence. The women quoted in this chapter will help us become more sensitive to the accumulation of fear and shame that can occur when a mother doesn't embrace the emotional and biologic growth in her daughter to which Pipher refers. We have a role to play in our daughters' personal and social expectations, and in that role we can be of profound help to them in reducing any guilt and shame they may feel about their bodies and sexuality, or, we can facilitate predictable pain. The journal *Behaviour Research & Therapy* reported the devastating consequences of guilt and shame being affixed to a girl's sexuality: "Whereas guilt reflects a feeling that one has done something bad, shame focuses not on the act but on the self; one is something bad. Shame is extremely debilitating because it's the entire self that is painfully scrutinized and negatively evaluated."[2] Maybe our own mothers didn't have the social support to have mediated shame for us when we were young, but now, through identification with other women's stories, we can feel supported in heeding the call for confidence on our daughters' behalf.

HOW FAR WE HAVEN'T COME

If we learn how to become women in the context of other women, what happens when a girl doesn't have a mother, or maternal figure? And if a girl gets her first period with no understanding of it whatsoever, what might it feel like to her? In my field, psychology, once you've observed an extreme version of a personality trait you can more easily detect aspects of it in the general population. So to illuminate how important it is to have a sense of belonging to our own gender through our connection to our mothers, I include a narrative completely absent of a maternal presence. It will show us how it would feel for a girl to go it alone. This is the story told to me by a spirited 71-year-old woman named Ruth who lost her mother when she was a baby and was raised by her abusive father. The story she shares with us takes place right after her father has remarried and her new stepmother has just moved in.

> I had just turned 12. The day before I started I was feeling under the weather and I was told to watch what I ate and not overeat. That night my father and stepmother were out for the evening and my older brother and I were home alone. He was downstairs studying; I was upstairs in bed listening to A Date with Judy on the radio. Suddenly I realized that I was damp between my legs. I went into the bathroom and discovered I was red on my upper legs. I was wearing red and white striped pajamas and the first thought that came to mind was, did I urinate and did the colors bleed? I cleaned myself up, put a pair of underpants on, and because the pajamas were hardly damp, I put them on also. I finished listening to the show, and the next one was Calling Henry Aldrich. During the commercial break I noticed I was feeling damp again. I went back to the bathroom and discovered my underpants were red. I couldn't understand what was happening, and all I could think was that maybe I had wiped

myself too hard. I stood up and got the Band-Aids from the medicine cabinet, but couldn't figure out where the Band-Aids should go. I put a couple on anyway. I was frightened. My brother called up and wondered why I was walking around when I should have been in bed. I wanted to tell him, but I didn't want him to come and look. Again, later that night, I went to examine myself and the bleeding was more profuse, and now I was really scared. I had no answer for why this was going on. There was nothing in my mind to explain it. I took off the pajamas as well as the underpants, and put on another pair of underpants before I went to bed, praying that I wouldn't bleed out and die. I fell asleep and woke up in a pool of blood the next morning. Usually when I awoke I jumped out of bed and got ready for the day. This day, I just laid as still as I could so I wouldn't bleed any more profusely.

As Ruth told me her story, her memory was visceral for her. A little girl all alone, lying as still as she could in a pool of her own blood, waiting to die.

Her experience is the extreme. But shockingly, many of today's young women are looking back and finding that they were subject to remnants of the same emotions Ruth felt; they experienced elements of fear and confusion while being denied the maternal warmth to tie it all together. In describing it in my study they use adjectives like *alarming, shameful, horrible,* and *dirty.* Their mothers may have been in their lives physically, but in terms of providing comfort and a sense of belonging they were absent. These daughters, much like Ruth, were largely left on their own to try to make sense of their emergent sexuality.

Psychologist Barbara Marcus writes, "Absence of a mother's affirmation of her daughter's body, both its appearance and its unique abilities, figures prominently in a daughter's problematic relationship to her sexual self."[3] With the onset of menstruation, when our daughters' bodies and emotional lives begin their shift into adulthood, they need us to prepare and reassure them so they can gradually assimilate a respect for themselves as women. We don't have to embellish, leading them to believe violets will flow from their uteruses and bluebirds will serenade them five days out of every month; we can leave that sort of thing to the people at Disney. What we do need to teach them is how remarkable the female body is—not only in its reproductive capacities, but in its supreme influence over the emotional texture that often distinguishes us from men. We need to make sure they know that their female bodies are something to be revered. If we do this, as teens they'll feel they have our support through the transition into adulthood, and as adult women it will be easier for them to have a comfort with their bodies and erotic lives. If we don't guide them, as we'll learn in the following chapters, many of them will live lives dragged down by poor body image, sexual ignorance, and sexual disappointment.

THE PAWNING OFF OF OUR DAUGHTERS' SEX ED

Many of us try to take steps toward educating our daughters, and while that's a great start, there's more we could be doing. As the following quotes will reveal, daughters notice our emotional and informational retreat around menstruation. They're very clear on our reluctance to give them helpful information over time in a useful manner. If we were to think of it in terms of teaching them how to build a fire, it's like we give them a piece of kindling, and then hope their school or a book or their friends will give them the rest of the materials they need. But what ends up happening is they only get one piece of kindling from each source and they're left with nothing of substance to take the process any further. They get a bit from us, a bit from sex ed, and a bit from other places—but none of it is enough to keep a fire going. They're left with a sorry little bundle of twigs (bits of dry information), no wood (helpful, contextualized, and ongoing information available anytime from the mother), and no match (a mother's emotional support and love).

In my study, women of all ages confided that, upon reflection, they saw their first period as an emblem of distance between them and their mothers. To give you a sense of how this happened, especially in the younger set, where we might not have expected it, the following seven women (a 19-year-old, five women in their twenties, and one 32-year-old) tell their stories. All of them learned about menstruation in school or catch-as-catch-can. Their comments echo experiences of other women from the study, ones that cut a demographically wide swath among African American, Hispanic, Caucasian, straight, gay, and bisexual women of different religious beliefs, educational backgrounds, professions, and states of residence. Given this range, their stories can't be dismissed as an anomaly.

I got my period and changed my underwear at least six times before I found the nerve to tell my mother. When I told her she gave me a pad and that was it. Physically it was painful with cramping, and emotionally it was completely empty.

* * *

I wish my mother had told me more. I was scared to even tell her when it happened. I didn't know what it was at first. One day I was nauseous and the next day there was stuff in my underwear. I thought I was sick but took care of it myself. It wasn't till it happened again the next month that I realized [what it was]. I think I was pretty strong to handle it myself. I thought I would cry or be upset but instead I just pushed on.

* * *

I wish my mother or one of my many aunts had helped me. I was very nervous about it. It happened at night. I was 12 years old and really afraid. I remember going into my mother's room, waiting for her to get out of the shower and being afraid that she would be mad at me.

* * *

I wish it had been handled more in the home as opposed to the school.

* * *

I was very frightened. Even though I was 13 and knew it would happen eventually, it was really scary when I saw blood in my underwear. I just wish I hadn't felt so alone because I probably wouldn't have been so scared.

* * *

[The biology of] it was imparted to me in sex ed class...it was never something that I'd discussed in any real way with anyone, especially an adult figure. [When I got it] I felt like I had done something WRONG! I was so scared, as though if anyone found out about it I would get in trouble.

*   *   *

I think of it as yet another experience that perhaps my mother could have used to bond with me that she did not.

Because of its ordinary nature as a bodily function, there's an almost mundane quality to menstruation. But what interested me in the responses from women ages 18 to 105 was that 60 percent of them wished they'd been taught about it differently. And this is what appears to be the essence of that sentiment: At its heart, our initiation to menstruation has largely to do with the quality of our mother-daughter relationships. If a mother is completely cold and withholding or cruel her daughter will feel abandoned, and the relationship may be at risk of significant damage. If a mother only imparts a little information, her daughter will probably resent the lack of support and connection but be grateful for what little she was given, although she'll be less likely to confide in her mother any troubles she may have relating to her body or sexual relationships down the road. But if a mother uses menstruation as an opportunity to deepen her closeness with her daughter, her daughter will come to trust her all the more and develop a confidence that, no matter what issues she may face in her life, her relationship with her mother will always be a soft place to land. Daughters appreciate when their movement into new womanhood is acknowledged and somehow celebrated by their mothers. It means a lot to them that we care about what they're going through and when we provide this warm attention. And as I'll show in later chapters, this is especially important around trauma.

Respondents in my study did include reports of mothers who really came through for them around the life change of menstruation, but for most, even when daughters were taught about it by their mothers, it wasn't necessarily satisfying, and many daughters were left completely on their own, or their education on the subject was farmed out to other sources entirely. Yes, sex education should be taught in schools. But school courses are there to augment us, not replace us. We need to be teaching our daughters about their bodies at home from the time they're little, so they're used to it being a part of our relationship with them, rather than waiting until their adolescence, when the information will feel forced and outside the bounds of what we usually discuss with them. If we normalize discussions of sexual development in the home as they're growing up, with each conversation we're actually normalizing *their* sexuality for them. But if we perpetuate shame in the home through our silence, avoidance, or rejection of their sexuality, we're actually gradually immersing them in a shame they'll carry with them throughout their lives.

Psychologically speaking, the parts of our past that hold memories of some kind of tension usually link to the discomfort we experience in the present. This is the psychological dynamic at play for a girl who gets messages from her mother that her menstruation is somehow dirty. If her mother doesn't teach her about it; if she primarily uses it as an opening to introduce negativity (as in, "don't ever let boys play with you down there"); or if she conveys that menstruation is a humiliation, then menarche—the portal to adult sexuality—will become corrupted by dirtiness and its companion, shame. This will in turn create some kind of tension in her daughter's life. The *Journal of Sex Research* shows data from dozens of clinicians supporting the following argument, which lays out how this biological and sexual pathologizing occurs.

> Although menstruation is a natural reproductive process, it bears a strong cultural taboo that commands that it not be seen, discussed, or in most ways, acknowledged....This desire to keep menstruation secret is often paired with an attitude that menstruation is dirty and disgusting....Shame about menstruation is often extended to the vagina and its surrounding areas, which are considered by many women to be unspeakable and unpleasant. . . [and

women] spoke of menarche as an experience that "contaminated" their bodies and their genitals in particular...Because menstruation and sexual activity often share the same intimate location on women's bodies, shame regarding menstruation might influence a woman's general approach to her sexuality. Furthermore, girls are often socialized to connect menstruation with sexuality.[4]

A girl whose mother never talked about anything to do with sexual development; or who was abrupt with her daughter when she was doing something all children do, like touching themselves; or who humiliated her daughter for her natural human curiosity will gradually attach a sense of dirtiness to her own body. A daughter can't menstruate and be *truly* comfortable in her own body if she believes her mother sees her sexual development as dirty, because this would mean that her mother sees *her* as dirty. And consciously or unconsciously she'll understand that this makes her mother dirty too. She'll arrive at this conclusion by simple deductive "if, then" reasoning. A daughter reasons: if my mother is idealizable, and I am like her, then I too am idealizable. On the other hand, if my mother is less than idealizable, and I am like her, then I too am less than idealizable. Phyllis Tyson writes in the *Journal of the American Psychoanalytic Association* that a "girl's idealization of her mother often entails a wish for a fantasized, idealized relationship with her in which there is a sense of oneness...[and] when anger at the mother is intense, it not only disrupts a sense of intimacy and interferes with the girl's self-esteem, it may also interfere with her pleasure in being female like her mother."[5] Here, Tyson isn't implying the mother needs to be perfect, or that the daughter can't express healthy anger at her mother, but rather that a daughter desires a mother she can look up to, and if the mother repeatedly fails her, she will experience conscious or unconscious anger toward her mother for disappointing her in this significant way. The disappointment and anger will obstruct the daughter's ability to respect her mother, her connection to her mother, and therefore, to her self. Tyson underscores how important it is for a daughter to have an ongoing positive identification with a mother who can raise her with the ability to value herself not only as a person but as a female, which includes her body image and her sexuality. In the psychoanalytic school of thought, Self Psychology, founder Heinz Kohut considers this one of the most important elements of personality development. Healthy idealization has the same effect on humans that sun has on a plant. The psychodynamic functions attached to what he terms the idealized self-object and merger with the idealized self-object[6] operate by a principal of growing into oneself through the nurturance of an idealized figure of safety and strength. This is a safety we all crave: feeling a oneness with someone we admire. And none of us would want to feel a oneness with someone we don't hold in esteem, because we could never feel good about ourselves. Knowing this will help us be more proactive in revealing a sense of value in ourselves and offering it up to share with our daughters.

If a mother lacks this confidence in her own value, the odds will be against her daughter because she'll in all likelihood grow into a woman who has difficulty feeling confident in her body, and since she'll spend her entire life living in that body, this is a huge deal. It will be the body she makes love in, the body she goes to work in, the body she socializes in, the body she raises her children in—and this lack of body confidence will contaminate her sense of herself in far more areas than just her sexuality. Naturally, this is not at all what mothers intend. So even though these things are hard for us to think about, being aware of the possible harm we might be doing our daughters presents us with the exciting and empowering ability to change the course of their lives for the better. The more we value them at home, the more confident they'll be as they go out into the world and face the challenges it presents women.

A study in the journal *Gender and Psychoanalysis* by Daphne DeMarneffe, in which she interviewed preschool-aged children and their parents about their understanding of sexual differences and sexual anatomy, found that girls are more likely to have been taught the word "penis" than *any* specific word for their own genitals.[7] It's with this sort of educational slight that sexist attitudes brew in our homes. When we don't teach our daughters the names of their genitals, not only does it make it that much harder for girls to have a growing understanding of them, it disavows our girls of any appreciation of them. An easily rectified problem such as this begins to build the very shame and ignorance that keeps sexism afloat. If a boy has a penis and a girl has a "down there," healthy views of female anatomy and sexuality are handicapped from the start. (One might argue that that is because the penis is external and the vagina internal. However, the vulva is just as externally apparent as the penis, and because we were never taught the correct names for our anatomy, millions of grown women still mistakenly refer to our vulvas as vaginas.) According to Justin Richardson of Columbia University and Cornell University and Mark Schuster of UCLA, in their book *Everything You Never Wanted Your Kids to Know about Sex (but Were Afraid They'd Ask)*, no age is too young to start teaching both sexes about their genitals.[8]

Unconscious sexism in our homes is of course directly correlated with sexism in society. The lack of a true acceptance of female sexuality in the United States continues to make it difficult for women to feel equal with men, and we're contributing to this unevenness. In our families, when our daughters are young, it may be experienced as "boys have a penis; girls have a 'down there.' " When they're women, the discrimination carries on in a broader context. After his release from prison for helping mastermind the Watergate break-in, G. Gordon Liddy returned to us in the form of a radio talk show host for Radio America. On the *G. Gordon Liddy Show* in 2009, nationally broadcast and available on SIRIUS and XM radio, speaking as a uniquely qualified champion of justice, he aired his concerns about Judge Sonia Sotomayor's suitability for the U.S. Supreme Court: "Let's hope that the key conferences aren't when she's menstruating or something, or just before she's going to menstruate. That would really be bad. Lord knows what we would get then."[9] Another example would be President George Bush's Right of Conscience Regulation, which, according to historian Barbara Berg, even though the American Academy of Pediatrics urged against it, broadened the definition of abortion to include many kinds of birth control, especially oral and emergency contraception, and allowing health care providers to withhold available medical information if it conflicts with their moral or religious beliefs....Those on the right claim they're honoring... the sanctity of motherhood, but their real beef is the freedom birth control affords women to enjoy a healthy, safe sex life while avoiding unwanted pregnancies. That speaks to forty-two million—or seven out of ten—American women in their childbearing years who are sexually active and don't want to get pregnant.[10]

We hold the key to making it so much easier for our daughters to fight these inequities. A girl's sense of who she is in the world is developed in her home. If her sexual sense of herself is grounded in that home through a positive attachment to her mother, whom she recognizes as a sexual being just like her, she won't ever have to worry that her mother will judge her for her biological functions or for being sexual, or worse yet, fear she'll lose her mother's love if she acts on her natural sexual inclinations. When a daughter internalizes part of her mother's own sexual comfort it pollinates confidence in the daughter, who will then go on to be less susceptible to the pressures of negative views of female sexuality out in the world. It's impossible for women not to absorb our culture's archaic take on how and when and with whom we should use our bodies. But if we expose our daughters to our strengths rather than our fears, our desire for their confidence will be what they assimilate into how they see themselves.

It's disheartening that in our supposedly postfeminist society, where a woman's education can lead her to fulfill a dream of flying into space, many of us aren't educating our daughters on the things that are useful for them to know for life right here on the planet. As a culture we continue to celebrate women as sexual objects and still struggle with letting women be subjects of their own sexuality, which Deborah Tolman of Wellesley College and the Center for Research on Gender and Sexuality defines as "a person's experience of herself as a sexual being, who feels entitled to sexual pleasure and sexual safety, who makes active sexual choices, and who has an identity as a sexual being."[11] The culture at large doesn't make it easy for women to have a sense of ownership over our bodies, but we can challenge this by changing the ways we perpetuate this unfairness in our relationships with our daughters.

In the *Psychology of Women Quarterly*, T. A. Roberts, using what is called objectification theory, connects the dots between the cultural objectification of women and women's personal internalization of this objectification. She writes that in our patriarchal society, which sexually objectifies women, female bodies have to be clean and pure, and that menstruation most of all, must be hidden.

> This emphasis on cleanliness is especially evident in the cultural discourse surrounding menstruation.... Objectification theory posits that the cultural milieu of sexual objectification functions to socialize girls and women to, at some level, treat themselves as objects to be evaluated based on appearance. The theory argues that girls and women come to internalize an objectifying observer's perspective on their own bodies, becoming preoccupied with their own physical appearance, as a way of anticipating and controlling their treatment in the world—an effect termed self-objectification....[W]omen's practices of self-objectification involve a kind of psychic distancing from their physical bodies. That is... the more women internalize a sexually objectifying standard on their bodies (viewing their body as an outside observer, engaging in chronic surveillance of their appearance, experiencing body shame) the more they appear to hold negative attitudes and emotions toward one of their bodies' most obviously physical functions: menstruation.

Roberts also cites a 2002 study in which a woman in the presence of a wrapped tampon was found to cause both men and women to see her as less competent and likeable. The study subjects also felt the need to move away from her. Roberts alludes to this study to shed light on the bind women are in. In order to not be judged, we avoid discussing or revealing menstruation.[12]

This is how sexism seeps into the mother-daughter relationship. Culture rains down on us shameful messages about menstruation, we unconsciously absorb them, and the runoff reaches our daughters. Our society makes us uncomfortable with the subject, and that discomfort inhibits our ability to reach out to try to change things for our daughters. We're not teaching them to understand their bodies, and they're afraid to come to us for help. But maybe we shouldn't be surprised. They sense our discomfort, and sometimes they learn not to come to us because we teach them they shouldn't. Although we love them, many of us have been avoiding the subject of sexuality from the beginning, long before our daughters' adolescence began to inch near, and when that time finally does arrive, we follow suit and add menstruation to the list of things we dodge.

Because no woman ever taught us how to go about it, even if we do try talking to our daughters about sexual matters, it can still feel like scary business, so we do it in a quick, detached manner. Like an inoculation. Or a drive-by shooting. In all of these ways we risk sending our daughters messages that foster shame. Mothers don't avoid or fear things that are normal and healthy, and our daughters know this. They take in our direct and indirect lessons that sexuality and menstruation are somehow disgusting and not good. Otherwise, why wouldn't we teach them about these issues just like we teach them about everything else? What this means is we're making our shame and dread, not our daughters, our priority.

We're putting our own fears ahead of our daughters' well-being, and we have to confront this crisis of confidence in order to offer our girls more grounding in sexual vitality than we were given by our own mothers. Otherwise, what's really happening is that instead of facing our own fears we're enlisting our daughters to help us carry the burden of them. The Women's Realities Study respondents expressed the same theme repeatedly in numerous questionnaire topics: Over time the unintentionally shaming messages we mothers share with our daughters accumulate to become so heavy that they weigh down our daughters' spirit and weaken our relationships with them. We are their role models, so why should we make them take care of our emotional needs rather than the other way around? They sense our fear, and they protect us by not making waves for us. Knowing we were too uncomfortable to teach them about their anatomy and menstruation, when it comes time to consider other things like intercourse, oral sex, or the complexities of desire, they'll be unlikely to challenge us to go even further outside our comfort zone because they won't want to be let down. They'll stop asking questions and stop coming to us for guidance because we've given them the message that we can't handle it—like the late bloomer quoted at the beginning of this chapter who was so upset by her mother's silence she didn't even bother to tell her mother when she finally got her period, and like Anne, in the case study in this book's Introduction, who gave up ever asking her mother for help again after her sophomore year of college. Our daughters' disappointment in us causes them to lose faith in us; and when they lose faith in us, they by extension lose it in themselves.

With regard to menstruation, our reluctance to shake our own sexual concerns gets in the way of our being our daughters' allies, because sexuality is inherently a piece of the mother-daughter relationship, and we need to realize it's often an index into other intimate areas. If they feel our neglect around menstruation, they'll likely feel it in other spheres, either because we actually do let them down or because they're so used to it happening they anticipate it will again. This has the power to bring about complex emotions that daughters might have to weather throughout their lives—feelings as rough as betrayal: *I felt betrayed because my mother should have prepared me for this. I was very young to start, yet she should have seen the signs.* It can also cultivate a sense of self-loathing that makes it easy for these girls to grow into women who feel disconnected from their bodies. I would argue that this disconnection begins in part with the disconnection they feel from us. We instigate it. If we're disconnected from even talking about the bodies we share with them as females, how on earth can our daughters not feel disconnection when they actually want to use them? Two women in their late twenties to mid-thirties testify:

My parents handled it all so poorly—it's really, really shocking. I was completely mortified of my body—for most of my life—and it totally started me on a path of disconnection with my sexuality.

* * *

I have been disconnected from my body and my sexuality for much of my life. The indoctrination I received set the tone for a sense of shame and guilt about it that lasted until much, much later in life.

Our inability to confront our own sexual issues can also leave our daughters feeling abandoned by us as this 43-year-old woman illustrates:

I wouldn't have known it then, but [her not teaching me about menstruation] was one of the first of many life-altering moments in which my mother left me out there all alone. Shaming my loss of virginity, denying me at 20 when I asked her to take me to get a diaphragm, being jealous when I fell in love. My first period was much more about my relationship with my mother than about my relationship with my body.

Based on the Women's Realities Study findings, I would take it even one step further: Our relationship with our bodies *is* about our relationship with our mothers.

If menstruation is seen as the gateway to womanhood, yet mothers are uncomfortable with it, as evidenced by their avoidance of discussing it with their daughters, then what does this tell us about ourselves? I believe menstruation, this seemingly mundane condition of being female, hints at the fissures in our core vulnerability: we're not fully comfortable welcoming our girls into womanhood because we ourselves aren't fully permitted to be comfortable there.

EMOTIONALLY, IT WAS A BEREFT EXPERIENCE

My mom explained what would happen and why... but never covered the emotional part of it. I wish she would have asked more how I felt about it and encouraged me to talk about it. I was at summer camp. I was embarrassed. And embarrassed to tell my mom.

This young woman addresses the importance of keeping the door of emotional connection to our daughters open. Her mother talked to her, yes, but their conversation lacked a soothing emotional quality and the daughter was left wanting more. Enough was missing to leave her with a residue of embarrassment that then led her to maintain whatever distance or disconnect she felt from her mother. The result is that they drifted slightly apart at a pivotal time in the daughter's life, when what she yearned for was the opposite.

Her example teaches us that even if the emotion a daughter struggles with isn't as bold as full-on fear, the other feelings she might be processing—like embarrassment—only add to the upheaval of having her body change before her very eyes. As mothers, our objective isn't to make things harder for them, but sometimes we unwittingly do...even mothers such as the one in this young woman's story, who *did* take the time to speak to her daughter. Because we're not supported by society, and because of the trepidation we've inherited from our own mothers' handling of things, we're flying blind when it comes to how to be there in a fuller way for our girls. If we're reluctant to teach them the anatomical facts of menstruation, it stands to reason that taking on the emotional side, which was never modeled for us either, is daunting. But if we understand that the emotional piece has value, and that our daughters *want* it, we'll be able to offer it to them much more comfortably. And even if we do offer some education, the process of helping them understand menstruation and sexual maturing involves far more than a five-minute lecture and a diagram of their reproductive system. If we're less rushed and antiseptic when we teach them, we can create space for feelings to emerge. Our emotions influence everything in our lives, but they hold a distinctive position in menstruation. Of course our daughters need to have an intellectual understanding of how their bodies work, but as any woman who's ever found herself in a fevered pitch of outsized emotions during her cycle knows, menstruation is not an intellectual sport. Even after several decades of practice I still think to myself when my period comes, "Oh, *that* explains my little episode last week..." So for the young woman quoted above, embarrassment isn't an intellectual experience, it's an emotional response she feels alone with. When a mother leaves emotional explanations and a sense of emotional closeness out of conversations with her daughter, then naturally when the daughter feels an emotion that fell through the cracks of her mother's teaching, she has to figure it out on her own. And one of the things she's left to sort out is why she feels embarrassed to talk to her mother.

It's not that we as mothers want to interfere and impede our daughters' ability to learn how to work through their emotions on their own, but that we should try not to exacerbate what they might already be up against. As women quoted in this book have told us, first periods can be scary. A girl goes from living in a carefree body to finding herself in a new one that demands her attention in ways that feel completely foreign to her. Since the seismic hormonal shifts that occur in the early years of menstruation often create intense emotional states girls have no experience in handling, it seems unnecessarily cold not to do our best to soften the blow for them. Yes, menstruation has a what's-the-big-deal side—we all do it—but the adjustments it ushers in for first-timers are too big to take in all at once, and sometimes mothers forget that. One woman nailed it when she said, *It was a very tough time, and I really didn't want to grow up.* This was echoed in a casual conversation I had with an eighth grader while we were sitting next to each other at a soccer game a while ago. She told me she was fine with her mother talking to her about menstruation in the years before she got her first period. "Now," she said, "I don't want to hear anything about it. I hate it! I like to pretend it's not even real. I hate that it makes me all moody, I hate the feeling sick part, my hips have changed and clothes feel different....So far? I hate being a woman." Her description of making the shift from having menstruation be a nonthreatening *idea* in the years before it starts, to what it feels like to be *living* through it can help us remember how overwhelming it can be. This is why pediatricians, therapists, and sex educators all advocate beginning kids' education when they're young. It helps them gradually build a secure base from which they can begin to tackle the rougher times they might encounter. Getting used to a new period is already a lot to take in—if our daughters are in the dark about what's happening to them, or feel left alone with it, it's even harder. Giving them the information in the years before they will need it ensures they'll have it when the time comes. It will also allow us to give them the windows of privacy and space they may need if talking about it while they're in the throes of going through it for the first few times feels too overwhelming for them.

If we can make our daughters wear bicycle helmets to protect their heads, then we can offer them our openness to cushion their emotions. When the emotional ground between a mother and daughter isn't crossed, both lose out on the richness they could have enjoyed there. This loss is noted by the following two women, aged 19 and 51, respectively, as they reveal how a lack of closeness with their mothers influenced their desire to do it differently with their own daughters. Since they're more than 30 years apart in age, taken together, they track three generations' worth of attempts to tackle the topic of menstruation. The 19-year-old shares how she imagines she would talk to her daughter about menstruation if she has one.

I was told the mechanics of it—what to do when it happened (i.e., how to use pads), why it happened and what changes in our bodies it signaled. The female teacher who first gave us the talk...was very straightforward about it. The school nurse repeated the lecture almost to the word, but I remember her seeming awfully embarrassed about the whole thing. I do wish that my mother had given me the talk too, but our relationship isn't really one where we talk about these things. I think I would have benefited immensely from knowing a bit more about the emotional side of things, and what to expect other than physically....I think I would explain [it to my daughter] by telling her about the development in the human body as we grow older. I would want for her to know my own experience with it, and how it has changed me emotionally and, more than anything, make sure she trusts me enough to tell me and share her own rite of passage.

Through her words we can see how the more removed mode of learning from school professionals, albeit useful, would differ from the more intimate help a girl might be more fortunate to get from her mother. She missed out on the nuance a mother could have provided, and, as we can see, her desire for that emotional attachment will inform how she'd raise a daughter. "More than anything" she would want her daughter to be able to trust in her emotional availability.

The 51-year-old woman took her memory of how she felt learning about menstruation with other girls in health class and used it to provide her own daughter with a richer experience that included a maternal bond:

[When I was young] we muddled through. At least we had "facts." Emotionally it was a bereft experience. [But] ah! My daughter began her cycle in earnest as mine ended. She was very easygoing about asking me for information. The information was always part of talking about being female, all her life, so it entered her brain at different phases and probably meant different things to her. Her school has a very extensive life skills program and she brought home lots of info on puberty and menses during her sixth, seven, and eighth grade years. The classes were blended, so the girls learned about boys' puberty as well. Pretty cool, I thought. She took responsibility for her own menses very well, until she tackled tampons (to make it easier to do her dance classes and swimming). She asked me for information and was freaked out about inserting the tampon. It took a few weeks and several boxes of tampons for her to reach a comfort level. Now it is old hat.

She was pleased to have the school supplement what she'd already taught her daughter at home. And you can hear her enjoyment in gradually bringing her daughter into a growing awareness of her body. It was an effort they shared—a partnership in growth—especially as one entered menstruation and the other menopause.

Both of these stories are proof that our yearning for closeness can be just as much of a motivator in how we approach the emergence of adult sexuality in our daughters as the fear we'll do something wrong.

WHY BOOKS ALONE AREN'T ENOUGH

Lots of the mothers of my study respondents gave their daughters books on menstruation. Very few of them had conversations about them. Daughters described these books mysteriously appearing on their beds or in their underwear drawers—like top-secret information passed off by a special strain of spies who only executed their missions during school hours. While this was especially true of women over 40, it happened to the younger generations too. Women reported that there was either no discussion of the book, or only some brief reference to its content. *I was given a book and was told to read it and if I had any questions to ask!* was a typical report of the experience, as was, *I was given a book...by my mother. There was no talk accompanying it, as I remember. I was given the book when I was about 9 years old and that was that.* It was also common for girls to try to cobble together information from a composite of sources, like this woman who says she got *a lot from reading Judy Blume books. And some furtive chatting with equally clueless friends. Some info from my mother, but don't remember anything substantive there.*

When we're frightened enough to resort to subterfuge or elliptical communication, our daughters learn to accommodate our reticence by forsaking their right to know how women work. They learn to retreat inward rather than come to us, and then the same cycle our own mothers were introduced to by their mothers gets carried on through us. But if we start reading some of the age-appropriate books (like *It's Perfectly Normal*[13]) with them when they're eight or nine, they'll know we can continue to help them with their understanding of things as they mature. They'll trust we'll provide them with new information as they're ready, and they'll know they can come to us with any questions they might have because we've already proven to them we're up to the challenge.

We forget how dizzying it can be when it's all so new. The unfamiliar sensations, the paraphernalia, what it all means.... The following vignette is engaging because it reveals how elaborate our understanding of what menstruation is can be—even for girls who go through it fairly smoothly. This woman looks back on her own first period as fairly uneventful, but notice everything she observes swirling around her:

I was one of millions of girls who read Are You There, God? It's Me, Margaret. *I knew I was (supposed) to be thrilled to get my period while simultaneously being embarrassed by it. Quite the paradox. I knew it was (supposed) to be a pain all around: that I'd be a bitch, that I'd cry uncontrollably and scream at people. This I got in no uncertain terms from Pamprin and Midol commercials. I was going to swell, bloat, and be unhappy, and that men and boys would shun me if they knew I was menstruating. That's what I (thought) I knew before I started. I had my first period on New Year's Day of 1979. I was thirteen. I admit it was anticlimactic. It did not bring with it my long hoped for breasts. It was a bit of a smear on a tissue for a couple of days and that was about it. My mom said, "Well, you're a woman now." Don't get me wrong, I was glad to have passed through the gates of biological childhood, but it was really no big deal. My cousin, though, quaked in fear and loathing when she got hers. She panicked and just cried and cried. I felt sorry for her because she claimed she felt dirty.*

HOW DAUGHTERS WISH THEIR MOTHERS HAD TAUGHT THEM ABOUT MENSTRUATION

I'll let these women speak for themselves:

I wish my mom would have told me all the details before it happened rather than afterwards.

* * *

I wish my mom would have talked to me about it before it happened. Even though I knew a lot…I think it would have opened up the lines of communication between us.

* * *

I wish my mother had been more comfortable with her body and been able to instill that in me.

* * *

I wish my mother had had the courage to tell me about my steps toward womanhood.

* * *

I wish my mother had been stronger and more communicative.

* * *

I wish it had been taught to me in a way that made me excited and proud rather than anxious.

* * *

I do wish my mom had spoken to me about it. Not because I needed the information but because I craved to bond with her as a woman and as her daughter.

* * *

I wish my mother would have discussed it as a rite of passage. And, even though I might not have been in the mood to have celebrated, she would have taken the challenge to make me feel good about it.

* * *

It would have been nice if my mother would have explained what was happening to my body biologically and my emotions that accompanied the period. But, she probably didn't explain anything to me because she didn't really know herself.

We have on average 13 years from our daughters' birth to prepare for their menstruation. In addition to working toward protecting our relationships with them, and doing our best to inspire the assimilation of a healthy sense of sexuality into their identities, there is much research that indicates that if we don't help them get a sound sexual footing they'll be at risk in concrete ways, in addition to emotional ones. Menstrual and genital shame are linked to feelings of disgust and self-loathing, decreased sexual satisfaction, and increased sexual risk-taking. Not having been taught to focus on her own body, a daughter will instead focus on her partner's judgments and sexual wishes rather than her own desires or safety which will make it more difficult for her to protect herself from subjugation, violence, infection, and unintended pregnancy.[14] So to motivate us, here are three positive vignettes that can encourage us to go through this educational process along with them, rather than leaving them—and us—to go through it alone.

I liked my mother's model of talking about it normally, for as long as I can remember. It was never something mysterious or scary because it was something she talked about.

* * *

I really liked the first period, because it was special as the first time, the mysterious thought of being a woman. I remember lying awake the whole night, and feeling proud of myself and special. Being part of a club, where I couldn't enter before.

* * *

I have a seven-year-old daughter who is already aware that I have a period having come in and out of the bathroom while I change my pad. In fact, when she was younger she called it my "pyramid." I've told her that women have periods, and she knows that she will, too, one day. As she ages, I' ll discuss more of the experience with her in as normal a manner as possible. We've actually raised our son, who is five, in a similar way... aware that the box of pads under the sink is for Mommy's period and ready to discuss it along with all of the other usual things like hygiene and homework and appropriate behavior as his age and capacity dictates. These are all ongoing discussions for parents with their children as opposed to a singular talk.

THE HISTORY OF SHAME AND SEXISM AROUND MENSTRUATION

The terms *feminism* and *sexism* don't always go over well with younger women, who might see them as symbolic of angry women with an ax to grind, or as yesterday's issues. That's one of the reasons I'm going to take us all the way back to 1952, to a book written by a man two decades before the second wave of feminism. Princeton social biologist and anthropologist Ashley Montagu's classic *The Natural Superiority of Women*, which presented scientific evidence for gender equality, argued almost 60 years ago for an end to the problems young women in my study continue to face.

When I was in college I had the pleasure of meeting the author one summer while I was working in a bookstore at Chautauqua Institution. He was in his mid-seventies and we sat together on the plaza outside the store for a weekend of book signing while he was on tour with a different book. At the end of the weekend he won my heart when he signed a copy of *The Natural Superiority of Women*, which is dedicated to his wife, for me and said in a tender and not-at-all-creepy way, "Ah...If I were but 50 years younger, ours would have been a great romance!" We went on to be pen-pals for a while, and whenever I think of him, I remember a man who genuinely respected and appreciated women.

A social scientist of the caliber of Margaret Mead, Montagu championed the betterment not of mankind but of humankind; and to do this he used anthropological evidence to correct the cultural misperception that men were biologically better, stronger and smarter than women. His research concludes that women are biologically superior, in that we are best able to promote survival of the species: "Superiority in any trait, whether biological or social, is measured by the extent to which that trait confers survival benefits upon the person and the group."[15]

The history he unearths on the shaming of menstruation begins with men's frustration that they can't bear children. According to Montagu, in order to assuage their feelings that they're biologically inferior to women in this way, he asserts that men, in an effort to devalue this ability in women, turned menstruation and child rearing into a handicap.

"Ludicrous as the idea may appear to some, the fact is that men have been jealous of women's ability to give birth...and they have envied their ability to menstruate; but men have not been content with turning these capacities into disabilities, for they have surrounded the one with hand-icapping rituals and the other with taboos that in most cases amount to punishments."[16] Nowhere is this dynamic more clear, he says, than in the Old Testament creation story in which it is Adam who gives birth to Eve.

He goes on to explain, "One can deny the virtues of women's advantages by treating them as disadvantage and by investing them with mysterious or dangerous properties. By making women objects of fear and something to be avoided as unclean, one can lower the cultural status of women by simple inversion. Their biological advantages are demoted to the status of cultural disadvantages."[17]

In addition to testifying to men's attempts to elevate their stature by demoting women, he cites another compelling reason for men to shame menstruation and childbirth: Doubt about paternity. When women are reined in by shame and disability they are easier to keep in line.

The fifth edition of The Natural Superiority of Women came out in 1999, shortly before Montagu's death, and was well reviewed for having remained relevant, and for the accuracy of its conclusions, as borne out by modern research technologies, such as brain imaging, not yet invented at the time of its first publication. Ten years later, in 2009, knowing I would want to buy it for my daughter, a friend of mine turned me on to a new book written by a young woman on her way to her freshman year of college. Rachel Kauder Nalebuff's anthology of first-period stories, *My Little Red Book*, went on to be a bestseller. However, in a book review for *The New York Times*, Alexandra Jacobs wrote, "The news that someone has published a bunch of women's memories of their first menstrual period is bound to provoke snickers, if not sneers....What's next, a collection of ruminative essays about bowel movements?"[18] In fairness, her review was more neutral than negative. She said she found the book to be distinctive and noted that it was interesting that Kauder Nalebuff's stories reveal that daughters weren't given much information by their mothers. But the tone of her review reflects the unconscious shame we've been lugging around for forever. It was originally foisted on us by men, but now we've become complicit in accepting it. As mothers at this time in history, we have a choice. We can continue to say to our girls as they grow into women, "Come up here and scrunch under this glass ceiling with me." Or we can say to them, "Let me break this ceiling so when you come up here with me, we can stand up straight under the open sky."

A REPORT FROM OUR SISTERS IN THE FIELD

A few years ago I had occasion to be hanging out with two of my favorite sixth-grade girls while I had a coffee and they sipped chocolate drinks the consistency of wet concrete. I wanted to hear what preparing for adolescence was like for them, and they agreed to be quoted on the condition of "like, total anonymity." I asked how they felt learning about menstruation, and in a mixture of giggling, gravity, and eye rolling, this is what our sisters in the field had to report. One said, "No offense, but sometimes what I read about it is cheesy. If I talk to my mom, I like her to talk to me one day, then *stop*...then wait for me to come back if I have questions." The second said, "I *love* talking to my mom. . . but not for, like, *hours and hours and hours and hours!* " What they wanted was a balance of closeness and independence, and information dispensed to them bit by bit, with time to make it their own.

Every mother-daughter relationship is different, and for those that are lacking, thank God for girlfriends and literature written on our behalf. There are obviously many helpful ways to approach the topic of menstruation, but maybe the best place to start is thinking of it as part of a lifelong dialogue between mothers and daughters, and between women—old and new.

Our support of our daughters' menstruation is crucial to strengthening their ability to feel proud of, and centered in, their sexual identities. Three women from my practice will give us just a taste of what we're up against, and why we need to do whatever we can to help our daughters build an unshakable sense of themselves.

Christine, a 56-year-old woman who raised three children who are now off on their own, has been divorced for over a year. Having been monogamous since she married in her twenties, much of her session time is spent wondering if she'll ever find love again. She talks a lot about how important her sexual energy is to her, and how much she misses that side of herself. After dating a few men she didn't particularly click with, she meets a Mr. Wonderful and is elated to feel alive in her desire and her desirability again. When we explore whether she feels ready to be with him sexually, she tells me, "I am. But I don't want him to think I'm a slut."

Six months into our work together, a 38-year-old investment banker starts her session with an announcement. "Well, Joyce, I was a big fat whore last night." I cock my head at her statement, because since her last relationship ended almost two years before, she's been hoping to meet a great guy, and one has finally come along. She, like Christine, has spent hours making it clear that being in a relationship would be really meaningful to her. She's a progressive woman who's wanted a sexual coupling, and now she's apparently had one. "What happened?" I ask. She grins. "I slept with him." "Did you want to?" Her grin widens. *Oh. Yes.* "So what's whorish about following through on something that you know is meaningful to you?" Her answer? A genuinely reflective "I don't know." She can't explain why she feels like a whore when, rationally, she knows that all she did was act on her desire as she had been hoping to.

Lastly, a 24-year-old assistant editor is at a party and runs into the guy she's had a crush on since their junior year of college. They've always had a good connection, but tonight she's over the moon because he's flirting with her. It's been a long time since she's been with someone she felt sexually attracted to, and the entire evening she's hoping they'll leave together. The gods shine down upon her and a plan to leave together is made. She's thrilled. But she demands they exit through the back door so her friends don't see. "Why?" I ask. "I don't want them to think I'm a skank."*

In 1942 the highly regarded doctor and psychoanalyst Clara Thompson published an article, "Cultural Pressures in the Psychology of Women," in which she observed, "The cultural attitude about the sexual life of women has been one of denial. In former years there was denial almost of its very existence. Today there is still the same tendency to deny that it is as important or urgent as the sexual life of men."[19]

And today in my practice, three women—one who came of age during the free-love era of the 1970s, the second from the generation that benefited from the freedoms won during that period, and the third representative of the more recent hook-up generation—all feeling the exact same fear. Each of them knows in her heart what's important to her but also understands there are consequences for women who follow their human nature. How can it be that these women who cover more than 30 years of modern "progress" meet the same discriminatory and unjust fate that "Gammy," the 105-year-old we met in the Introduction, would have met at the turn of the twentieth century?

---

* I feel compelled at this point to say that the truly promiscuous behavior that unfortunately earns a girl or woman the label "slut," "whore," or "skank" is usually a symptom of someone who has been sexually abused, raped, emotionally abused, or neglected. In other cases it can be a sign of mental illness, such as bipolar disorder. When these terms are thrown around casually in our vernacular they disregard the severe misfortune of girls and women who are trying, in the ways they know how, to feel either loved, in control, or sane.

I believe this is a fate we can help our daughters avoid...or at very least fiercely combat. What a grown woman comes to feel about her body, and worries other people are going to judge her for, springs in part from what she learned from the tone of her relationship with her mother. We need to try not to inadvertently discriminate against our daughters' sexual development because we've become so accustomed to facing it ourselves that we don't even notice it anymore. Instead of setting our daughters up for the clean girl/dirty girl or good girl/bad girl split, we can encourage their cognitive and sexual cohesion. It will be much harder for our daughters to ever think of themselves as sluts if they know their sexuality has our respect. If we don't teach them the names of their body parts when they're little, respect their curiosity about sexuality as they grow, and teach them how to be attuned to their bodies in adolescence, how do we expect them to feel respected enough to have the emotional presence to hold their own against social stigmatizing? And if we stigmatize their bodies, how could they arrive anywhere else but a place of shaky self-knowledge? We need to help them know themselves. And we need to let them in enough to know us. If we don't, what we cultivate is distance and ignorance.

Modern Mothering

Chapter Three

Letting Our Daughters See Us as Sexual Women

I think it's funny that women, who are supposed to be the great communicating sex, really don't share that much in this area. We have a LOT to learn from each other about our bodies in regards to sex, sexuality, pregnancy, birth, breastfeeding, menopause... everything. Things we all share but never REALLY talk about.

*I*n my study, the third most popular questionnaire topic, after menstruation and relationship with your mother, was, quite surprisingly, masturbation. "How about that?" you might be thinking, as I did when the results came in. Women wanted to explore the most personal aspect of their erotic lives—the sexual connection to the self— and were curious to know how other women experienced the same. The masturbation questionnaire was more popular by far than any of the others on sexuality, all of which were partner oriented, and it contained one of the only two questions in the entire study to get close to having a unanimous response. Not only that—this particular question was also the most emphatically answered of the nearly 1,200 questions in the whole study. And here it is: *If this survey were to be published, would you want to hear other women's thoughts and feelings on masturbation?* Ninety percent of the women reported a strong desire, answering "yes!!!" and "absolutely!!"—sometimes with one to three exclamations points for emphasis! Out of 63 topics to choose from, why were women of all ages drawn to these three as the ones they most wanted to talk about and learn more about from each other? And what could masturbation possibly have in common with menstruation and our mothers? The answer is that each has to do with an aspiration to better understand what it means to be female—to have a sense of belonging with our gender. And women need information from each other in order to accomplish this. One of the reasons we need to pursue this sexual material with each other is because our mothers, our female archetypes who haven't been supported in their own sexuality, weren't always as forthcoming with it as women would have liked.

Masturbation is a private topic women are inclined to keep secret because we feel it's too personal to share, which is understandable. The disadvantage of this secrecy, however, is that it creates a silence in our dialogue with each other, which inhibits the sharing of knowledge, experience, and information. Without this exchange, including the passage of information from mother to daughter, the shame and guilt accompanying masturbation will be more easily propelled into the next generation. My research indicates that women didn't necessarily want to hear about their mother's masturbation—once again we feel the presence of The Ick Factor—but, women did wish that their mothers had presented it to them as normal and as a way to explore their bodies. The spirit of the respondents' intention to pursue and share knowledge on masturbation didn't read as exhibitionistic or voyeuristic but rather as a drive to feel a sense of community. The language one woman used to describe this spirit was *I'm certain I'd feel less alone.* Another said, *I want to know if there is anyone else who feels the way I do, and what does she do about it?* Most were willing to reach out even under their own resistance, as one woman captured when she said, *I felt a little embarrassed answering #17*—"How do you typically masturbate, and what are the qualities of this experience, physically and emotionally, that make it your preferred way?"—*but if the information helps someone else, then I'm glad I did.* Their responses contained a balance between a need to protect highly intimate confessions and a wish to reach out, connect, and learn.

This echoes the balance most of us strive for in our mother-daughter relationships. What do we keep private and what do we share as we try to find the best proportion of healthy interdependence to autonomy? Since our first experience of female identification and belonging begins with our mothers, and because our sexual development takes place under their auspices, our sexual senses of self commingle. Taken together, what women have to say on menstruation, masturbation, and mothers expresses a longing for an expedition into our sexual selves and how they are intertwined with our mothers.

Women who completed the masturbation questionnaire ranged in age from 18 to 66, with 85 percent of them identifying as heterosexual, 10 percent as bisexual, and 5 percent as homosexual. (Responses showed no discernable patterns of difference between the orientations, so I haven't drawn distinctions between them in my analysis here beyond a couple of observations included in the sections on fantasies and orgasm that follow.) One of the most striking things women revealed was that almost everyone who chose to respond to this questionnaire confessed that she did so in spite of the fact that it made her uncomfortable. They didn't do it because it was easy. They did it because it was important to them. So in this chapter, we're going to explore our sexuality through the prism of masturbation. I hope that learning the psychological and emotional value of masturbation from these women, who discuss its present role in their lives as well as reflect on it when they were girls, will offer women some of the information and sense of belonging they crave. It will help us feel a new level of comfort with our own sexuality so that we can teach our daughters about theirs with the confidence many of us wish our mothers had had.

WOMEN WANT TO TALK ABOUT MASTURBATION, THE CORNERSTONE OF HUMAN SEXUALITY

Masturbation—defined in the study as the act of touching yourself when you are alone—is the perfect starting point for us to examine our sexuality as a whole. This is true for several reasons. First, the masturbation questionnaire was the one in which women were the most forthcoming about the component parts of their sexuality and sensuality. Despite whatever discomfort they felt in responding, they were generous in giving the physical and emotional content of their experience because they wanted to share it with other women. Second, masturbation is the earliest exploration that occurs in human sexuality, though it's not sexual in the way an adult would experience it, so for many it's the most long-standing part of our sexuality. It can begin in infancy and is commonly observed by the time children are toddlers,[1] so many women have a story line of masturbation that runs through their lives, like the 38-year-old teacher who reported,

> I am most comfortable getting on top of and rubbing up against a pillow. When I was very little, I used to play boyfriend and girlfriend with a friend. We used to "hump" each other as part of the game....We learned quickly not to tell anyone that we played this game and eventually stopped. I began to continue doing it on my own, thus masturbating from a very early age and not really understanding what I was doing....I have never changed how I masturbate after all these years.

Her narrative illustrates the arc of our sexual development as well as our personalization of it as we each have our own memories, experiences, and preferences. And the third reason masturbation is the perfect starting point for us to examine our sexuality as a whole is that it is the simplest way for women to get a sense of what feels good sexually: when engaging in it we're not distracted by the physical and emotional complications of partnered sex. This is especially important because, as a study in the *Journal of Sex and Marital Therapy* finds, women reported often being preoccupied during sex with self-conscious thoughts or worries about their partner, for example, "I worry the whole time my partner will get turned off by my body without clothes" and "While... with a partner, I think way too much about the way I am moving."[2] Or, as one young woman from my study said in response to the question, "Is there anything, physical or emotional, that you feel during masturbation that you wish you felt during sex?" *Comfort. I can make whatever face I want, twitch wherever I want....Sex requires a little acting, smoke machines, and hocus pocus.*

Many of us believe women have come far sexually, yet what women had to say about masturbation in the study is jarring in how it questions that progress. Catholic, Jewish, Protestant, atheist and agnostic, Buddhist—even a Quaker, a pagan, and a Wiccan—Asian American, African American, Caucasian, and Hispanic, all women wanted the same thing. They wanted to talk about it, write about it, and learn how other women felt about it. But only under the protection of anonymity. In their real lives most didn't talk about it at all, and only a few would give it even a brief mention with friends. Although women reported feeling liberated in being able to write about masturbation in my study, the topic is still so taboo they nevertheless reported discomfort talking about it anonymously! This was reflected in responses from college-age women, *I imagine other women were just as uncomfortable as I was answering these questions. Because this topic is not talked about, none of us know what the norm is, so our answers may be completely strange for all we know;* to women in their thirties, *I am still a bit uncomfortable. Like I am doing something wrong;* to women in their sixties, *Feels a little personal. I'm not that comfortable answering all the questions.* If we as grown women don't feel comfortable talking about it, even when we're voluntarily choosing to on the privacy of our home (work or library) computers with complete anonymity, how can we encourage our daughters to feel comfortable? One-quarter of the women who completed the masturbation questionnaire said they wouldn't teach their daughters about masturbation, and of those women, only one cited a reason even remotely to do with a daughter. The most common responses from the rest of the women were *I wouldn't know how* and *I don't know if I would be comfortable enough to do it.*

Women responded on the topic of masturbation because it was something they not only wanted to talk about within the safety of their anonymity but because they were starving to hear other women's thoughts and feelings on it. Because of its private nature, they cited a lack of material and conversation that left many of them feeling uncertain about where they fell in the spectrum of behavior. Their responses revealed what they needed: a confirmation from *other women* that they were normal, not alone, and allowed the fullness of what it means to be sexual beings.

THE PSYCHOLOGICAL AND EMOTIONAL
FUNCTIONS OF MASTURBATION

In an effort to learn about human sexuality, masturbatory behavior has been studied by researchers, most famously in our culture, by Kinsey[3] and later by Masters and Johnson[4] in the 1950s and 1960s. Erotic guides for masturbation that include cultural histories in an attempt to undo pathologizing social convention have been written to promote sexual enlightenment and happiness in women.[5] And medically, when coupled with orgasm, masturbation's physical benefits, like maintaining vaginal tissue, which can atrophy without the blood flow involved in arousal, have been touted by OB/GYNs and urologists such as Christiane Northrup[6] and Jennifer Berman.[7] Its ability to also reduce pelvic and back menstrual cramping has been documented by a report out of the Department of Biomedical Science in the UK.[8] And according to *The Science of Orgasm*, sex researchers from Rutgers University even report that orgasm and masturbation play roles in achieving less stress and lower rates of heart disease, breast cancer, and endometriosis.[9] On the mental front, psychoanalytic literature on masturbation began with Freud's assertion that it caused neurosis,[10] but as research advanced that theory was rejected and it became accepted as a part of normal development by developmental theorists such as W. R. D. Fairbairn and Margaret Mahler.[11] However, while today's therapists accept masturbation as a part of sexual self-knowledge and a contribution to better partnered sex, not much has been written on the psychological and emotional meaning of it to women and the way we use it in our lives beyond the purpose of sexual gratification.

Broadening our definition of masturbation to include its psychological and emotional contributions to our lives will enhance its meaning in our collective consciousness and therefore make it easier to appreciate and talk about, especially with our daughters. Women from the Women's Realities Study have offered their experience to this end.

EXCITEMENT AND SELF-SOOTHING

When asked when they tended to masturbate, in what state of mind or mood, or to cite what was usually going on for them in the moments before, most women said they tended to masturbate when they went to bed either to release the day's stress or to wind down before falling asleep. They used it to transition from busy to restful. *At night before I go to bed, usually in a self-indulgent, happy mood. In the moments before, I'm usually just breathing deeply and enjoying my bed. It takes me less than a minute usually. I hope to feel like I'm treating myself, the same way I might feel when I get a pedicure.* Some used it as a means of easing into the day. *Usually the mood strikes when I wake up after my husband has left for work....I know I have to get up soon, but I just really want to enjoy those last few minutes in bed. Plus, the orgasm helps wake me up, since I'm not a morning person.* Coffee will forever pale in comparison. Through these two ways of using masturbation it's easy to trace its soothing functions back to earlier ones like the lullaby that sends an infant off to sleep or a mother's delicate stroking of her child's hair to rouse her awake after a nap. They represent masturbation's ability to adjust energy and comfort levels necessary to wind down or wind up.

Many women reported masturbating at work as represented by these two quotes. *When I've been crazed I've even done it at work in the bathroom or in my office with the door shut, after everyone else has left for the day.* And, *Anytime. Morning, before work, at work with door shut, at night. Funny, but it's rarely in my bed.* Some masturbated in their cars, and one 53-year-old said, *I always get horny when traveling, especially on a plane. Sometimes, when I emerge from the bathroom I would wonder if the other people around me could tell.*

This one act women rarely speak of beyond a quick reference is capable of serving many emotional and physical purposes. There's a lot of talk about the mysteries of female desire, but we seldom ask what prompts women to stimulate themselves sexually. Whether it's emotional, visual, or sensory, there's always something internal going on for us before we masturbate. What might psychologically and emotionally precede arousal for women?

If we speculate on what might be happening with one of the women who masturbates at work, she could simply be thinking of something arousing, but her masturbation might also relieve her boredom, or it might serve as a distraction from what she ought to be doing. Maybe she lets her arousal into the workspace to make it more her own, more under her control. Maybe she feels powerful there and titillation celebrates that, or maybe she doesn't feel so great at work, and titillation rescues her. Maybe she's so sidetracked by what her body needs she feels she has to masturbate in order to be able focus on her work. And how about the woman on the plane? Does she masturbate because she's turned on by the excitement of travel, or is it about sharing a huge space with strangers who don't know anything about her so she's released from all of the things that usually define her? Or is it possible she finds herself in a sexual zone because it distracts her from her fear of flying?

Whatever the case, the business of masturbation is streamlined for productivity because all we require is our body, so our ability to masturbate goes anywhere we go. Just like a baby's thumb, it's right there whenever we need it. These women's quotes are important because they remind us of the ongoing moment-to-moment nature of our sexuality. It's alive and dynamic. Just as our mental activity isn't restricted to the classroom, sexual expression isn't restricted to the bedroom.

EXPLORING FANTASIES

Fantasy affords a different way to reach into ourselves to find a semblance of being with someone we'd fancy. We can be soothed by the fantasy alone or use it to inspire us to inch closer to taking real steps to actualize it. One woman said, *I love to fantasize. As a married woman I would never cheat because I am very happy with my husband, but using a fantasy lets me live out those lusty feelings we all get towards other people.* Another married woman who identified as heterosexual used fantasy too, but to imagine being with a same-sex partner: *I always fantasize about a black woman giving me oral sex.* And when asked if there was anything she felt during masturbation that she wished she felt during sex, a third woman who also referred to herself as heterosexual said, *Yes, an attraction to the same sex, which I haven't experienced in real life.*

The latest sexual research on female desire finds that it isn't restricted to gender.[12] It's far more complex than male sexuality, and women's fantasies allow us the chance to appreciate any layer of that complexity we choose, which is incredibly freeing, given our culture's propensity to objectify and contain us. Each woman's fantasy life stakes a claim for her subjectivity and personal agency, which gives our lives more balance than our culture often permits. Respondents' comments epitomize fantasy as the playground of the mind, and because masturbation is accompanied by intense physical feeling as well as perhaps emotional ones, it isn't fantasy in black and white, it's fantasy in color.

COMFORT AND PRIVACY

While every woman loved the feeling of being intimate with a lover, masturbation held a special place of safety, control, and freedom.

> *I feel a bit freer, more able to connect to my fantasies better because there are no chaotic uncontrolled elements.*

*   *   *

> *Actually, it's what I don't feel during masturbation that I wish I didn't feel during sex, and that's the pressure to orgasm. When I'm touching myself, I'm not in my head about it. When someone else is touching me, I feel kinda under the gun to orgasm. . . which makes the experience not as pleasurable.*

There's a profound intimacy inherent in being alone with our thoughts, and when we combine it with the intense concentration on our bodies masturbation entails, it allows us be suspended from the restraints of the outside world for a few moments. For women who feel pressured to conduct themselves a certain way, like feeling the constraint to be nice, a complaint women in my practice regularly have, letting go is difficult.

If during masturbation a woman can be liberated from the pressure to conform to someone else's notion of what she should be, she can focus only on her body and the way it wants to move. It affords her an uncontaminated connection to her own instincts. As many women in the study said, it's a gift to the self. And we should value the importance of masturbation as it stands on its own, not only as a vehicle to improved partnered sex, because it's actually a vehicle to the self.

ORGASM

I didn't include a question specifically on orgasm in the masturbation questionnaire, but here is a sample of what women had to say in response to a question regarding masturbation in the orgasm questionnaire. The question was "How would you describe the difference between orgasm with a partner and orgasm through masturbation? And do you have a preference?"

Some women found that climaxing with men involves a challenge that masturbation doesn't present. A 19-year-old bisexual mother said, *With a partner is soo much better, but guys are hopeless.* While a straight woman put it this way, *[I prefer] masturbation...I know how to do it. With a partner, I've only had a handful who can do it for me. I know myself better no matter how much I try to explain what they need to do.* Other women preferred orgasms that came from partnered sex due to the emotional engines that helped to drive it: *Orgasm through masturbation seems to me dulled in comparison to orgasm with my partner, probably because of the lack of shared passion. I much prefer it with a partner.* And some women loved both. *The orgasms I give myself are usually better, as I know where and how to touch. But there is so much more to sex than just the orgasm...both sex with a partner and masturbation are indispensable!*

Most women disclosed focusing more on their clitorises than their vaginas during masturbation because they often found them to be underutilized in partnered sex. This was particularly true of heterosexual women. As we can hear in both the masturbation and orgasm responses, women sometimes feel their partners don't have the proficiency they hoped for, but women are also aware they often play a part in inhibiting an improvement in this area. Many reported a reluctance to instruct, a proclivity for being distracted with self-consciousness, and a realization that they aren't as in touch with their bodies as they would like to be, which makes communicating needs to a partner that much more difficult.

In terms of masturbation techniques, women covered the spectrum. They used clitoral and vaginal vibrators: *Usually I start with a very light touch, sometimes just one finger. I rub the whole vulva, until I get more and more excited, and then I just focus on the clit, rubbing faster and harder. I also like to use a vibrator sometimes. With the vibrator, I feel like I orgasm harder with less work, but with my hands, I feel more emotionally in touch with myself.* They enjoyed vaginal and anal penetration, fingers, pillows, lubricants, fabric between their legs, and running water. They took in different kinds of porn and erotica, and they did it in a way that reflected their individual inclinations, as this woman humorously shares: *I read erotica or look at pornography. I prefer erotica because I feel more dignified somehow.* The use of fantasies and arousing material crossed sexual orientation boundaries: *I am heterosexual, but I usually masturbate using lesbian porn. Everything in this porn is centered around a woman's pleasure, which is something that never happens in my real-life sex life. Clitoral stimulation is my preferred physical method, as it is often ignored in the bedroom.* And this material also varied from romantic to different types of submission, *Usually laying on my back with my legs spread, spreading my labia with one hand, rubbing my clit with the other. Sometimes I use a small dildo for penetration. My fantasies always center around words. I concentrate on dirty phrases I want to hear that turn me on. I'm always in a pretty submissive role, but being really "slutty." That's just what works for me.*

In responding to this questionnaire, 22 percent of the women reported either very rare orgasms or not being able to orgasm at all, with most of these 22 percent being in their twenties. *I really want to. I try different things with my partner. I try to masturbate...but I don't know how. I was never taught and so I guess I have never orgasmed. Sex feels great, but I have never come to that point—and do not know how.* Another young woman's response highlights how the ability to achieve sexual pleasure has both emotional and social ramifications: *It makes me really sad sometimes to think about what I'm missing out on. I've tried a million things, and nothing has worked. I'm starting to think it's just not going to happen for me. When it comes up with my friends if I mention that I've never had one, they all look at me with pity and/or treat me like I'm a prude.* Many women in my study confessed feeling frustrated and alone with their difficulty orgasming, and it's my hope that women would be able to talk about it with each other without fear of judgment. To the question "Do you wish women would discuss orgasm more openly?" one woman in her early thirties answered, *Yes, I do because I thought I was a total freak for not being able to have orgasms with a partner for so long. I went my whole twenties thinking I would never experience this amazing thing that every woman I knew said she was experiencing regularly. But I, of course, because I was self-conscious, was lying and saying that I had them too. Now, in retrospect, I wonder if anyone else was also lying to appear normal.*

And lest we think women's sexual self-consciousness is confined to heterosexual sex, a young gay woman writes, *I think that recently I feel more free when I masturbate than when I'm with my partner. I don't feel as pressured to have an orgasm, so I do. With partners I feel like I have performance anxiety sometimes.* Meanwhile, a straight human resources director struggles with a similar distraction: *I would like to orgasm with my partner, but I'm too busy thinking about how to make the experience good for him. I put myself on the back burner.*

WHAT WOMEN WANT TO FEEL

As for the experience of masturbation itself, what did women say when asked to describe what they were hoping to feel? One described *a sense of release, followed by a sense of well-being and calmness [that] usually lasts anywhere between a few minutes to a day.* This woman teaches us how masturbation can go far beyond just "getting off." How many things are there in our day-to-day lives that can make us feel calm and full of well-being for an entire day? Masturbation, in response to whatever emotional/physical/ psychological impulse motivates her to engage in it, puts her into a mood that surpasses simply feeling good. Another woman expressed it similarly, drawing our attention to the power of self-care in any form and its ability to act as a soothing agent: *I always am looking to feel physical satisfaction, at which point I feel I have done something for myself which in turn creates this emotional comfort.* Emotional comfort also indicates something deeper than feeling good. Both of these women describe their experience as existing on a plane of emotional soundness, which tells us that the importance of masturbation extends far further into health than mere orgasm or a finding-your-inner-goddess vibe.

WHY MASTURBATION IS PART AND PARCEL OF OUR PHYSICAL, PSYCHOLOGICAL, AND EMOTIONAL DEVELOPMENT

When a mother holds her drowsy infant daughter against her shoulder, she'll soothe her to sleep with soft rhythmic pats to her tiny pillowy back, and when her daughter is five and falls off her bicycle, she'll kiss the boo-boo and rock her in her arms while gently whispering, "Sshhhh, sshhhh." These sensual and calming physical touches are the precursors to masturbation as we experience it throughout our lives.

Masturbation is the cornerstone of all sexuality because our understanding of adult arousal begins with the discovery of self-soothing when we're children. Our first sexual exploration is with ourselves. This fact is supported by the American Academy of Pediatrics, which pronounces it a normal part of development in both boys and girls, noting it's quite common especially in children under age five or six.[13] And the reality that infants are born inherently sexual is warmly described by Justin Richardson and Mark Schuster. To new parents they say,

> As you will soon discover, sexuality isn't created in a child by her first sex education class. Nor is it turned on by a single hormonal

switch that gets flipped at puberty...When you get a baby girl, the vulva is included, and even before she can speak she will discover that touching her genitals feels good. It looks like there's something sexual about that act, but full-fledged sexuality requires more than sensitive genitals. With time, this element will connect with other elements not available during infancy.[14]

The later elements Richardson and Schuster are referring to have to do with the maturation of sexual functioning that starts to become sexualized in an adult way during puberty, along with young adults' gradual cognitive and social development. Babies aren't interested in dating; teens are. To understand children's masturbation it's important to recognize that their goal is *soothing*, not *arousal*. Think of it this way: it's similar to a really common adult nonsexual behavior that's also masturbatory: playing with our hair. I can remember walking through my college library and noticing that about half the students would be twirling, pulling, or stroking their hair while they were studying. It feels nice. It's pleasant. But the students weren't doing it for arousal; they were doing it to enhance the calm needed to focus. So it is with children.

For teens and adults, on the other hand, masturbation is the sexual delivery method of excitement *and* self-soothing, and as the women quoted in this chapter show us, its functions are broad and powerful and uniquely designed by each woman to fit into her life. When we think of masturbation in children and preadolescent girls it's important to remember that this sexual self-discovery occurs on a continuum that runs through our life cycle. From infancy through old age, at each stage of life, its meaning to babies, girls, and young and older women will change because the life issues they're engaged in will change. For babies its meaning has to do with comfort, and for girls it may be uncovering the mystery of the changes they're experiencing in their growing bodies. For young women it may be about learning more about their sexual responses and determining what arouses them when they're alone versus when they're with a partner; while for women in their prime it might enable them to more deeply explore their sexuality to build on what they've already learned. And for older women, especially those who may have lost the sexual companionship of a partner to death or illness, masturbation may be their main source of erotic experience. All along the way, no matter the age, masturbation can promote sexual health and well-being in whatever way a girl or woman requires.

Deborah Roffman, who says that sexuality is about people, not body parts, is a sexuality and family life educator who has taught sex education in schools for 35 years. She further explains what sexual health is in her book *Sex and Sensibility* by sharing the philosophy of her school. Together with parents, teachers, and other adults from her school community, a definition for sexual health was written as a mission statement for the curriculum. Her "Philosophy of Sexual Health" includes:

- ❏ Enjoying pleasure and satisfaction from one's sexual experiences and feelings.
- ❏ Feeling a sense of comfort and fulfillment in one's gender.
- ❏ Participating in or refusing participation in sexual behaviors in accordance with a consciously evolving, internalized value system.
- ❏ Relating to others sexually in caring, supportive, and nonexploitive ways.
- ❏ Communicating comfortably and effectively about sexuality, both verbally and nonverbally.
- ❏ Taking responsibility for one's sexual behavior and its outcomes emotionally, physically, and interpersonally.
- ❏ Taking responsibility for one's sexual and reproductive rights and freedoms.[15]

As our daughters move through adolescence, a time when they're creating a social, physical, and emotional identity, masturbation can help them acquire a maturing sense of self. It can allow them to focus only on themselves and to feel ownership over their bodies, independently of partnered sex; it can connect them to their gender by including the touching of parts only belonging to girls and women; it can prepare them for the sharing of intimate knowledge required in a healthy sexual relationship; and it can help them to experiment through fantasy with what they feel in terms of desire. And, having already established the impossibility of separating personality and sexual development, we can say that these sexual senses of self can only enhance other aspects of experience, such as a well-rounded social ease, comfort with their own bodies, and a sense of what is emotionally important to them. Even in seemingly unrelated avenues of life these qualities have value. We don't tend to associate them with being a good mother, an effective manager of a Burger King, or the CEO of a corporation, but ease, confidence, and emotional self-awareness are all qualities that stand a person in good stead to be content and effective in the world. People who are well rounded tend to live well-adjusted lives.

In our effort to help our daughters have such well-rounded lives, we need to appreciate that if we don't support their sexuality their lives will likely be harder and less fulfilled. Deborah Tolman's study of girls and desire, conducted through the Center for Research on Women at Wellesley College, revealed that masturbation can augment a sense of confidence that keeps them grounded. One of the girls she interviewed captured this when she explained her belief that a girl's lack of ownership over her own sexuality contributes to her vulnerability and makes her more likely to engage in sex that isn't fulfilling because she doesn't know what she wants and will just do whatever peer pressure dictates.[16] This is another example of how sexual and personality development converge to build physical and mental health. A sense of ownership over one's body requires the same confidence as a sense of ownership over one's thoughts, perspectives, and behaviors. As confidence builds in one area it can be cross-referenced into others.

While Tolman worked with a socioeconomic mix in talking to teen-age girls, she found that for middle-class girls in particular the norms of femininity demand their bodies to be "'appropriately'silent."[17] She also found that while some girls said they would let another touch their body, masturbation felt alien to them. Of one of these girls she writes, "She is so accustomed to being the object of someone else's desire, 'allowing them to do things' to her, that exploring her sexuality on her own is not only a violation of femininity, it simply does not make sense."[18] Rationally, this is crazy and illogical. How could a member of the feminine sex touching her own body not be feminine by design? But the perils of the good girl-bad girl split reach into their emotions and mute them. Here we can see how women's sense of ownership over their bodies, supported by things such as masturbation, can address the problem of objectification that encourages the silence of their bodies. Recall that there is no bullet point for "appropriate silence" in Roffman's "Philosophy of Sexual Health."

* * *

The following vignettes offer windows into women's individual lived experience with masturbation. In each, I'll draw out features that might be of use to mothers who want to become more comfortable with their understanding of this aspect of erotic life in order to find it easier to support our daughters' sexuality as well as our own.

This college student directly sums up how some young women today feel about masturbation:

> Some of my friends will openly cry if you even bring up the subject, they are so scared. I believe girls my age think that there's something wrong with touching yourself. Some will only masturbate in the tub and let the water run because your fingers aren't actually down there. [As for my own masturbation] I have sex toys [and] I also enjoy just rubbing my clitoris with lubrication, but my all-time favorite is the bathtub; it's the heat. [Answering this questionnaire] feels freeing— first time you can openly tell all and feel like no one is sitting across from you judging, [and I want to hear other women's experiences] because it would be the truth and show that most of us have similar experiences....[I] wish it could be more celebrated."

She addresses the fear still attached to touching our own bodies, even going so far as to describe her girlfriends as scared by the subject. Is it wrong? Is it less dirty if we don't use our hands? But she also represents hope that we can move through our fears by talking about masturbation and seeing it as a sexual truth that unifies us and can be something to celebrate. And even as a young, liberated woman, she commemorates the experience of completing the questionnaire as the first time she's ever been able to explore her feelings about masturbation without worrying about being judged. Her story invites us to ask ourselves, as mothers, do we want our daughters to be scared of touching their own bodies, and scared to talk about it as girls and even as grown women? If the answer is no, we should open a dialogue and lead the way to their comfort.

Nathalie Bartle, like Tolman, found in her research on mothers and daughters that even girls who are having intercourse are uncomfortable with the idea of touching themselves. "Girls who spend hours in front of the mirror scrutinizing their appearances often have no idea what their genitals look like. Many girls believe it is more acceptable to be touched by a young man than to touch themselves."[19] She advises that mothers should level with their daughters and discuss and celebrate their sexuality, including masturbation, as "an important— and given—part of a woman's life" so that honest communication rather than shame becomes the standard.[20]

My mother was actually a proponent of masturbation. I think she believed it would keep me safe, especially because I came of sexual age when AIDS [was first coming to public awareness]. But I think masturbation is not generally accepted. [I experience guilt around masturbation because] sometimes my fantasies are quite self-deprecating and submissive. The act itself doesn't make me feel guilty. It's my fantasies. [In my preferred practice] I use my index finger to make circles on my clitoris. I usually lay or sit down. It is usually dark, private, and I can concentrate. [Answering these questions] I felt scared but brave. [I' d like to hear what other women think and feel], just out of curiosity. It would maybe help me know if I'm normal or not.

This woman's words give voice to our private need to feel normal. That she said she felt scared but brave completing the questionnaire shows us how ashamed we are about our bodily desires and the delicate precipice many of us are on: it requires bravery for women to fully embrace our sexuality, even in the privacy of our own minds. Shame is always accompanied by the dread of judgment, and here we see the unconscious at work, because intellectually we know sexuality is normal, but emotionally, the fear of being seen as abnormal creeps in to make us uncomfortable. Her story is also important because it shows how the pull of that dread makes it difficult to truly feel sexually healthy even when we've had our mother's support, as evidenced by her guilt over her fantasies of submission, for example.

With regard to such fantasies, it's important to understand why women might have them. Fantasies that involve things such as domination, violence, humiliation, and so on fill psychological needs we may have that relate to gaining or surrendering control. They can represent our wish to be found so desirable that someone has to have us no matter what it takes—even if it means breaking with social decorum or the laws of society. "The poetics of sex" therapist Esther Perel writes, "are often politically incorrect, thriving on power plays, role reversals, unfair advantages, imperious demands, seductive manipulations, and subtle cruelties."[21] In terms of safety, fantasies can also allow us to take a real-life violation we may have endured and rewrite it, or at very least, bring it into the realm of our own mind, thereby taking it away from the mind of whoever violated us, which can be healing and empowering.

One of the standard fantasies heard in psychological practice is of a woman imagining herself dominated. Being dominated is a way of relinquishing control, so if a woman prefers controlling her emotions, or if she's always in control at work, or managing her kids' schedules, organizing her life and the life of her family, then being dominated will be an appealing alternative. We hear of this with rich and powerful men who seek the company of dominatrixes—without this common fantasy, being a dominatrix wouldn't even exist as a career choice. Likewise for a woman who's always in charge, who would be uncomfortable being out of control in her regular day for fear some kind of anarchy would bubble up, in her fantasy life she can be relieved of all of that. If she's being dominated she has no choice but to comply. There are no decisions for her to make, no people for her to take care of, no distractions to take her away from the sexual task at hand. On the surface of the fantasy she may be tied up and gagged, but the psychological benefit underneath it may be that she can do nothing but accept the full force of sexual fulfillment. She is completely unable to do anything but feel the sensation of arousal.

If, on the opposite end of the spectrum, a woman's fantasies are violent, they could be offering her a chance to feel powerful and in control. If a woman has been a victim of some form of emotional, physical, or sexual abuse, a fantasy in which she's the perpetrator offers her the self-righting experience of being the one in control. Or if a woman feels generally powerless or invisible in her life, a sexual fantasy in which she inflicts pain on another might give her a way to experience having an irrefutably direct impact on someone. Even when our sexual fantasies are at odds with who we are in our regular daily life, they can still perform healthy functions. Fantasies always serve some psychological purpose, or else they wouldn't be in our minds in the first place. They're also like our dreams, and can be used for prescriptive purposes. They can often serve as a tap on the shoulder encouraging us to pay attention to something that needs tending to in our lives. If in our fantasies we require control, for example, we may want to see if there's any way to feel more in control of our real life so we can live with more equilibrium if we so choose.

I used to [feel guilt] because I started [masturbating] so young....When you're young you just know it feels good—you don't know what it looks like to those that are older. So my mom would get upset when I'd do it, and for a long time I had to sneak it, and through that, developed a negative connotation. With masturbation [I'm] only thinking about my own pleasure. When I'm with a guy I often shift to how is HE feeling, and therefore my orgasms during sex are few and far between. Which is a shame. My orgasm is just as important as his, but since I have for so long had such difficulty having a guy get me there I just forgo it, accept that I won't orgasm during sex, and just say I'll do it for myself later. Hmmm...something isn't right there?! [I typically masturbate] sitting down, with a piece of fabric pulled tight between my legs. [Completing these questions I felt] great. Why do I let myself, or the guy, off the hook so easily when I don't get off? I push my own needs aside—consciously too—because like so many women I aim to please...But I shouldn't do that.

When asked if she would like to hear other women's thoughts and feelings on self-stimulation, this woman answered,

Absolutely!!! It's not talked about nearly enough—at least not in my world.

A mother here has unknowingly forced her daughter's sexuality underground. A little girl who learns it's wrong to touch herself becomes a woman who has to struggle to focus on her own pleasure in her relationships. To me, this begs the question, if you've been made to feel uncomfortable touching your own body, how can you possibly feel comfortable letting someone else touch it, or showing them what you need?

The 16-to 18-year-old subjects of a British study, conducted at the University of Southampton, regarding young women's views on masturbation indirectly posed a different question. Do they even own their own bodies? One woman in particular captured this clearly. The authors said of her, "Stephanie spoke in terms of her body, especially her genital area, being almost property of boys—a place that only they could touch: 'I would never touch myself...you know...I think that's really disgusting...you know...it's just not right 'cos only a boy suppose [sic] to touch you there, and even then it's not that great [laughs].'"[22]

We've known for a long time that many girls have negative connections to their bodies, but this is another level of self-deprecation. It's an unconscious, culturally imposed disavowal of sexual ownership that leaves our girls as well as grown women with an underdeveloped entitlement to the rights and pleasures of their own bodies. This young Englishwoman's disconnection from her own genitals is so profound it's almost as if she leases them from young men as each sexual encounter demands.

From a focus on their partner's sexual satisfaction over their own, to a lack of ownership of their sexuality, the confidence we would want to see in other areas of our daughters' lives is sorely missing in the sexual realm. But thankfully, with simple interventions from us that support our daughters' sexual body integrity as they're growing up, it doesn't have to be this way.

Wrote one respondent in my study,

As a kid, we never would discuss [masturbation]. The boys always did, but we would deny we touched ourselves. Eventually that started to piss me off and I became something of a crusader for women to not only admit but be proud of the fact they touch themselves. I found that if I admitted it first, without any shame, the [other] girls would too. I really do wish girls could talk about it at a younger age. The boys didn't have the stigma, why should we? Why should I feel guilty? It's MY body!...Nobody has more right to touch me than me... not only that, but I'm better at it than anyone else is....More often than not I'm in the shower when I do it, simply because it's logical....I'm already naked....It only takes me about a minute to get it all done. Unless I've been drinking...then it takes longer....Until recently, sex wasn't about orgasm at all, seeing as I'd never achieved it....I had lots of books as a kid, given to me by my mother, that went into depth about sex and sexuality. I'm sure there was a chapter in there about masturbation, but reading about it like that didn't make it seem any more a part of normal sexuality. On the other hand, I remember my mother asking me AND my brother AT THE DINNER TABLE whether or not we touched ourselves. I wish the conversation had been ANYTHING but that. Typically, I'm relaxing in the shower....I usually start with some "foreplay" with the nipples and then just go for it, one-handed, on the clitoris. If I'm feeling saucy, I use the two-handed, one inside, one outside method.... . Physically and emotionally, I kinda look at it as a gift I give myself....I am unafraid and unashamed of masturbation. I only hope other women feel the same way!

This vignette holds out an alternative to many women's anxiety around masturbation. Instead of feeling paralyzed by shame, this woman uses her anger to confront the double standard. She realizes that if she took the shame out of her own masturbation, other girls/ women would open up too. In proudly admitting she masturbates, she offers the other girls social "permission" to feel less shame. This is a function mothers can provide for our daughters. We don't have to disclose our masturbatory techniques, but we can take the lead in giving them permission not to feel shame over their sexual agency.

This story can also serve to relieve mothers of the pressure to be perfect in our teaching of our daughters. We worry that if we don't do something perfectly we'll scar them for life. It looks as though this woman's mother gave her books but then didn't help her understand them, and that her mother's decision to explore masturbation over dinner rather than in a more sensitive way disturbed her daughter. But even though her mother didn't do it smoothly, she still managed to convey that it was nothing to be ashamed of, and she raised a daughter who feels confident. This is the power of normalization—it creates a bond—and we as mothers are in a position to offer this bond to our daughters.

EXPLORING OURSELVES

I wish I had known that I could have an orgasm right off the bat, I wish that someone had told me it is a good way to get to know my body and my sensuality. This woman's desire to have been taught about masturbation symbolizes its educative value and the way it takes us on a special voyage of our own bodies and our sensuality. How each of us would clarify the difference between sexuality and sensuality would likely be subjective, but for our use here, sexuality often contains sensuality, whereas sensuality doesn't have to contain sexuality. Sexuality involves the mechanical workings of the body, such as the swelling of the clitoris, and the other physical changes that come with arousal, including the brain's neurochemical role. Sensuality draws on all the senses, and includes an appreciation of things outside the body. The heat a woman feels in her vulva during arousal is sexual; the sensation of a bed sheet against her skin is sensual. Touch can be sexual, but the *way* we touch can be sensual. And many experiences are sensual without being sexual in nature. Whenever I zest a lemon, my eyes involuntarily close as soon as I breathe in the mist it releases. It's a sensual experience, and each such sensation invites an acknowledgment and confirmation that we are alive.

Deepening the appreciation of our sensuality augments our sexuality—learning our responses to touch, memory, and fantasy is crucial not only to developing an understanding of ourselves but in going on to share that knowledge of our bodies and hearts with a partner. The sexuality and sensuality of masturbation *enables* intimacy, and *enhances* it. It lets us practice, experiment with, and perfect listening to our own bodies to find what makes them stir, as these two study respondents revealed:

I just had my first orgasm with another person less than a year ago...I spent my entire twenties (including a marriage) not being able to come except when I was alone.... Before, it was all I knew about orgasming, but now I experience a whole new level of intensity with my partner....

* * *

I learned over the years that accepting pleasure is not a bad thing. Doesn't make me a bad person to pleasure myself. I've been single more than I've been in a relationship, so is the option, then, to deny myself physical pleasure? I don't think so. I've also become more comfortable with my body over the years, and exploring it has been enlightening—and tremendously helpful—for those few relationships I have been in.

Masturbation deepens our knowledge of ourselves as individuals by allowing us to gather uninterrupted data on our sexual response cycles. That requires an investment of time in ourselves, which can foster a growing respect that extends beyond arousal by sharing the same questions and answers we hold in other parts of our lives. What do I want? What do I choose to keep private? What do I choose to share? Why am I drawn to what I'm drawn to?

Sexual self-awareness informs other things we understand about ourselves because our sexuality isn't split off from the rest of who we are—from our personalities and the personal histories that forged them. Self-awareness in any area of our lives is important because it helps us make the informed decisions that stand the best chance of guiding us toward what we believe will bring us comfort.

THE IMMEDIACY OF SELF-KNOWLEDGE

Some women disclosed taking the time to savor the masturbation experience, as expressed in this delectable quote from a working mother in her early fifties: *I hope to feel orgasmic—the tension and release. I masturbate with multiple orgasms till I get bored or sore or someone comes home. An hour is average.* However, most women in describing their masturbation habits disclosed bringing themselves to climax surprisingly fast—within a minute to a few minutes. Given the interference of shame and guilt women confess, one might wonder whether this is representative of women feeling so uncomfortable arousing themselves that they rush through it. Whatever the reason, this capacity for immediacy is fascinating considering the attention given to women's arousal being more slow-paced than men's. Some of this disparity may be due to what Northwestern University professor of media studies Laura Kipnis refers to as "the whole vagina-clitoris fiasco...the placement of the clitoris, the primary locale of female pleasure, at some remove from the vagina, the primary locale of human sexual intercourse... not combined into one efficient package, as with the lucky male."[23] We all know there are lovers out there who just *do not* take direction well, but one prescription here is that if we can climax alone in 60 seconds, then if we speak up for what we need, offer instruction, and allow our bodies to move with another person the way we let them move when we're alone, we can maybe hold out hope that even the least inspired of lovers might help us get there within the hour.

It's our shame that holds us back from moving freely during sex, and sharing with our partner what we need. Letting our daughters discover and grow comfortable with which points of sensation feel good to them will save them from a fate women before them have suffered—relationships devoid of pleasure. A 65-year-old divorced editor captures the realities of living this way, writing that the most private things she and an adult girlfriend ever confided in each other were *that I'd never had an orgasm [and that] she didn't have sex when she was married—was still a virgin when she got divorced.* If we are open to letting our daughters be sexual creatures just as we are, they'll be able to experience both these slow-paced and immediate pleasures of intimacy without a chaser of guilt and lead happier lives.

FEELING CONNECTED

Women in my study reported that masturbation helped them feel connected to someone they cared for when they couldn't be with them, to ease the feeling of yearning. Self-stimulation is capable of achieving an immensely powerful connection to another. Music has the power to affect something similar in its ability to transport us mentally to whatever point in time we attach to a particular song. And dreams are magical enough to transport us in our sleep. But masturbation takes it even further by allowing longing to be *transformed* into physical sensation and physical memory experienced in the present. This makes masturbation stand out as uniquely transcendent, because it means the sensations and thoughts it creates make it perhaps the most complete way to feel close to someone who is absent—in other words, it might be the fullest way to conjure up the actual experience of being with another that a human being is capable of. To my knowledge no one has compared the psychological capacities of masturbation to that of music or dreams, or fantasies with sensation so intense you feel almost as if you're with the person you're fantasizing about. Only psychosis has the power to blend physical sensation with fantasy to that extent, but that of course falls under the category of hallucination and mental illness. Masturbation accomplishes all of this under the heading of fantasy and well-being.

Women use masturbation as the next best thing to being there or as a footbridge through the muck of being alone when you don't want to be. A 50-year-old professor writes,

> In the moments before, I am usually missing my lover. We rarely get to be together, and I feel overcome with love and nowhere to put it. Masturbation helps me quiet my longing by doing my best to feel close to him… by replicating how he makes me feel when we're making love. When I masturbate I'm soothed by the way my body reminds me of how it opens up for him, even when he's hundreds of miles away. The physical response to remembering how the weight of his body or his touch feels is what I want.

One woman told her story of using masturbation to help her cope with grieving the death of her lover. She described it as having brought on her most memorable and intense orgasm because of the crying it enabled her to release, as she missed him so much and felt his loss so deeply. She affirms masturbation as a means of coming to terms with loss. The stuff we don't talk about at funerals, but perhaps the most silently intimate part of bereavement. Looking at masturbation from the angle of a physical and emotional comfort to soothe bereavement can raise our respect for the deeply personal functions it fulfills. This can be especially pertinent for mothers. If our daughter were to grow up and lose the love of her life, we would never want her to feel guilt or shame for physically comforting herself in the throes of despair. But taboos on masturbation have precluded women from talking to each other about how we actually use it in our lives. If we raise our girls to experience negative feelings around masturbation, it will be nearly impossible for them to let go of the shame, even in situations such as this, when their need for comfort would be understandably desperate. Understanding the developmental line of self-stimulation will help us normalize it for our daughters and support their ability to live with the right to comfort themselves as they see fit throughout their lives without fearing moral judgment.

HEALING THE TRAUMA OF SEXUAL ABUSE AND RAPE

In my practice I often recommend masturbation for women who have had a sexual trauma. So much of the suffering they experience is about feeling a loss of control over the ownership and security of their bodies, and a woman can try to heal herself through two forms of intimacy. She can begin to renew herself in a sexual relationship where the healing comes from feeling safe *in her choice* to surrender some control to her partner. And she can begin to mend through masturbation, which gives her *complete control* over her sexuality— the chance to listen only to herself as she finds which sensations *safely* open her up to her own arousal.

To help us appreciate the coping required in the wake of sexual trauma I'm introducing, in addition to stories from cases in my practice, the comments of women who completed my study's rape and sexual abuse questionnaires. These women told their stories not only to help themselves heal, but also because they wanted to reach out to anyone who might be helped in hearing them. To honor them and their wish to do what they could to alleviate suffering in other women, here is what they, in addition to clients in my practice, have to teach us.

Sarah, a woman in her mid-twenties who worked as a television writer, was feeling guilty and angry because she was avoiding sex with her boyfriend. Every time he wanted to pleasure her orally she'd be overwhelmed by memories of having been raped by a man who had bitten and torn her labia. For her, the idea of surrendering control to her lover in this way was more than she could bear. Masturbation offered her an opportunity to try to reconnect with herself in a way that didn't involve being frightened or out of control. It also held out the possibility of gradually growing comfortable enough to be with her lover in a way that felt safe to her. We need to recognize that it's not only the touch of *another* that can be healing. Sarah's story elevates the importance of *one's own touch* to a level that's connected not only to the will to survive but the will to live a full and vibrant life.

It's also important to note that Sarah, because she was ashamed not of the violence of the rape but of the fact it was a sexual act of violence, made a conscious decision not to tell her mother she was raped because "I don't want her to think of me that way." She worried that it would be too upsetting for her mother and feared being seen by her as defiled. I have had other rape survivors say the same, and have had many women who were sexually abused as girls tell me they doubt their mothers would ever be there for them in the way they need. Emily, a 31-year-old financial analyst put it very clearly when she said, "Maybe she won't even believe me. She can't handle my having boyfriends let alone handle this. Then I'll have to take care of her...like that's going to help me."

There are other factors that can contribute to such a divide between mother and daughter—for example, an emotionally abusive or neglectful mother. But if reluctance to disclose trauma occurs in an otherwise healthy mother-daughter bond it could be because the mother hasn't set the stage for her daughter to confide the sexual content of her life, whether it be healthy or traumatic. As with grief, we would never as mothers choose to actively add a layer of shame to a tragedy, but Sarah's and Emily's stories reveal how it can happen without the mother ever knowing.

Recalls a young woman from my study who was raped by a close relative until she was seven, at which time he was incarcerated for the serial rape of women:

Being laid on the garage floor and having him put tools of various sorts inside of me. This was perhaps the scariest event, only happening a few times. Compared to the usual rape and molestation that occurred with him, it was much more painful and difficult to bear.

She told no one, including her mother, because, *I knew that telling would result in alienation from my family.* As for living with the effects of this as an adult, she writes,

> *When I go through periods of time that, for whatever reason, the abuse is on my mind more often, I recoil when touched, I feel jumpy, I check out during sex with my husband or avoid it all together. Sometimes a pain during sex, especially after childbirth, will trigger a memory and I feel scared while I am with my husband. I question myself, my ability to recall events accurately, and who I really am. Am I for use by someone else, or should I have a say in things? When I have a say about sexual matters, I often question it. If I don't feel like having sex, I feel like I'm letting my spouse down and think, "He shouldn't suffer because I am sexually abnormal," and I do it anyway with no regard for my own feelings. I can't tell when my lack of desire is related to my abuse and when it's just normal ups and downs.*

Another woman shares a somewhat similar story.

> *My grandfather would get into bed and tell me stories about when he was a prisoner of war and then he would fondle me. I don't remember everything. I would stare at the top bunk above me and disconnect from my body and kind of disappear. When I think about it, I either feel numb or I vomit. Everyone, including me, failed. I felt too much shame to assert myself and my needs. My mom seemed paralyzed by guilt. My dad, when my mom eventually told him, did nothing. My grandfather said I was a liar and a drunk when I confronted him….It seemed like no one knew what to do, and I stopped expecting support.*

In each of these stories we see daughters who had to worry about alienation from their mothers, or abandonment by them, or a fear of having to take care of their mother's emotions. Consequently, all of the daughters were left to move through their sexual trauma alone.

Two additional young women, each of whom was raped by her ex-boyfriend, describe what rape felt like to them. One reports

Suffocating terror. Abandonment from God. The deepest alone I have ever felt. I sometimes near this feeling during [the] panic attacks [I now have].

The second woman gives us inspiration to support our daughter's sexuality no matter what she may face, as she honors her mother for helping her save her life:

The police immediately dismissed my accusations because I waited one month to report (I was in an inpatient psych program for part of that month, trying to get myself stable) and [they said] that I likely was mad at my ex-boyfriend and wanted revenge. They also told me that when I stopped fighting him off, I gave consent to the act....For the first few days, I was very numb and just went through the motions of my life. Around the fourth day, I awoke and immediately felt the pain that I wanted to permanently end. I was so afraid of my emotions and my extreme desire to die, I turned to my mother for help. Had she not been there, I may not have made it through that day.

In 2008 the National Institute of Justice estimated that at least four hundred thousand rape kits are sitting untested in police stations and crime labs around the country, and a *Los Angeles Times* article chalked this up to an endemic disregard for women's safety.[24] The U.S. Department of Justice reports that somewhere between one in six and one in four women will be raped in her lifetime, and those statistics are based only on rapes that are reported. Estimates are that the real incidence of rape is even higher. And according to the U.S. Department of Health and Human Services there were more than seventy thousand substantiated cases of child sexual abuse in 2008.[25] This statistic, like those for rape, doesn't include crimes that are unreported. Of the women in my study, 73 percent of those sexually abused told no one, and only 18 percent of those raped reported it to the authorities. These figures also bear out the level of distress-driven secrecy I have found in my career as a private practitioner. For mothers, this means there's a probability our daughters could find themselves in a position to need us.

Sexual violence isn't something that's easy for us to think about. But I offer up these young women's narratives to jar us awake enough to want to do all that's in our power to let our daughters know we will always be there to honor and take care of them when they're in pain, and to do our best to raise them with the self-respect that will give them the surest footing possible, should they encounter the anguish of sexual crimes. One of the key markers of a daughter's self-respect is having been respected by her mother. A mother who listens to her daughter respectfully, and who respects her daughter's sexual integrity, is far likelier to raise a woman with a solid sense of self that can only benefit her ability to cope in a crisis.

There's an expression in child development that the last developmental milestone achieved will be the first lost to regression under stress. For example, if a child has just learned how to consistently use the toilet, under stress or trauma, she may regress and stop using it because she's overwhelmed, and psychologically needs to go back to the more certain ground of diapers. Physical health operates by a similar principle. If a woman's health is already compromised by a heart condition, and she has to have her appendix removed, her recovery will be at greater risk of complication because she was already in a weakened state. The same is true for the development of our sexual health. Without a secure baseline of sexual health and body confidence, if trauma occurs, and coping was already compromised in its development, then a girl or woman's ability to function will be even more impaired under the strain of assault. Rape and sexual abuse are hellish experiences to go through, but having a strong baseline of sexual health—which includes an appreciation of female sexuality, ownership over one's body, and the ability to engage in discussions around sexual matters without fear of being judged—will put one in the best possible position to heal.

If we set the stage for our daughters to know *unequivocally* that we are a safe haven and they truly can talk to us about *anything*, maybe they'll confide in us their need for comfort under strain. But if we've directly or indirectly made them feel shame about their sexuality their ability to weather catastrophe will be weakened. The stories of my clients Sarah and Emily and the women from my study exemplify the unhelpful sexual messages we can send our girls. They also reveal the resulting shame in themselves, and disappointment in us, that they carry into adulthood. Teaching our daughters about sexuality isn't a moral choice. It is done to help our daughters navigate their lives. When we teach them it's shameful to explore their bodies and we expose our own discomfort around healthy sexuality, we cannot expect them to believe we'll be there for them in a sexual crisis. If we want our daughters to know they can come to us with anything and they won't have to fear losing our love and respect, we have to earn that privilege.

THE GUILT BIND

Of the women in my study, 70 percent of them felt guilty about masturbating, and 80 percent of them were never taught about it as a normal aspect of human sexuality. This conflicts with what many of us believe: that we live in a modern society that benefits fully from sexual freedoms won by feminism's second wave. The upsetting truth is that shame, kept alive through sexism, retains its stronghold on our sexual sense of self. This is evidenced by the fact that a surprising 80 percent of these women are under the age of 35 and were raised by mothers of the postfeminist era.

Here is where the subtleties of sexism trip us up. Guilt has been so embedded in how our society views female sexuality that even women who intellectually reject it find it works its way into their psyches.

One woman said she didn't experience guilt around masturbation, writing, *Why should I feel guilt about doing something natural, that causes no harm or bad feeling. It's relaxing, and if we weren't supposed to enjoy sexual pleasure then why do we have a clitoris?* But she also showed ambivalence in the following response to the question of how she felt answering the masturbation questionnaire. *Sometimes I feel weird, and then I feel weird about feeling weird. I hate how repressed I feel sexually by feeling uncomfortable talking about something natural.*

Here we have what we've inherited. The struggle between wanting to feel free and comfortable with our sexual pleasure and still feeling caught on the snags of the notion that when it comes right down to it, only men deserve to move freely in their sexuality. We as mothers have tremendous power to help our daughters feel differently.

Sometimes this struggle for ownership of pleasure and relaxation can bleed even deeper into a personality or worldview.

When I'm bored or alone...I look at some porn on the Internet. Usually I am kind of excited about it, like I'm doing something "sinful" but really fun....I hope to feel physically good during [masturbation]....After is more complicated because sometimes I feel like I just wasted time and energy and nothing came out of it. Like I should have been doing something else, anything else "productive."...I just feel guilty about feeling good in general, about things that are not necessary or productive.

While this woman may have been referring to the work ethic with which she was raised, she also highlights a larger problem, which is women's relationship to feeling good.

Our society values women as caretakers—for what we give—and women often give to others before giving to ourselves, or at the expense of giving to ourselves. Masturbation, the definition of a woman giving to herself, strikes a lightning bolt into the hallowed ground of this value placement. Giving to the self isn't selfish. It's *self-sustaining*, and the psychological reality is, the more we give to ourselves the less resentful we are and the more we can give to others. In accepting that, we can accept masturbation as a productive function.

Another woman admits that she masturbates, but she and her friends don't discuss it. *I don't think we're comfortable enough to openly discuss said issue.* If she had a daughter she says she would never teach her about self-stimulation because *I don't know if I would be comfortable enough to do it* and added that in completing the questionnaire, *I blushed a few times and I imagine some other women might as well. I kept looking over my shoulder to see if anyone could read my answers.* Yet this woman said she would like to hear other women's different points of view on the topic. Another woman responded to the question "What do you hope to feel during and after masturbation?" *Less guilt. I have a bedside Bible that I usually stare at that might talk me out of it sometimes. Other times I try my best to avoid looking at it, and...*No one taught her about masturbation, and in response to the question asking what she would have wished such a conversation would have been like, she said, *If I knew how to make that into a normal conversation, I would have a solution to one of life's biggest questions.* Although she doesn't have a daughter she said she would not teach her about masturbation because she says she wouldn't know how to do so. Still another woman reported that *after [masturbation] I feel a mixture of shame and relaxation.* Although she wished someone had told her that *it was OK and nothing to be ashamed of* she wasn't sure she would teach her daughter when and if she had one. *It's a maybe. Kids learn so much from school that unless she asks it's not always needed.* And, just as the women previously cited, she went on to say she would like to hear other women's feelings on self-stimulation.

In the masturbation questionnaire it was noteworthy that so many women used almost exactly the same phrases when exploring the issue of guilt. They repeatedly asked: "Why should I feel guilty? I'm harming no one." In our culture, many women may feel this is the length we have to go to justify our right to pleasure. We can only have it if we can prove no harm is befalling anyone else.

* * *

Regardless of how 70 percent of the women in my study came by their guilt or discomfort, it's highly unlikely they wish to hear about other women's experience with masturbation because they're hoping to feel *more* guilt, *less* pleasure, and *less* permission to claim their human sexuality. They want to hear women say: It's OK for you to feel alive in these ways....I am like you and I want this for myself too.

That leaves us to contemplate an uncomfortable paradox: How can we wish for this for ourselves and not wish it for our daughters?

Remember that one-quarter of the women who completed this questionnaire wouldn't teach their daughters about masturbation, not because of anything having to do with their daughters, but because they were too uncomfortable with the topic and wouldn't know how. At the same time, 90 percent of these same women expressed wanting to learn more about it from other women themselves. Once again, just as it was with menstruation, we're putting our fears ahead of our daughters' well-being by making them take care of us, rather than the other way around. If even the women willing to explore their feelings about masturbation suffer from guilt, shame, and ambivalence when even thinking about it, what of the women who aren't that comfortable? And if even a quarter of the women who completed the questionnaire wouldn't teach their daughters what masturbation is, what of the women whose discomfort far exceeds theirs?

Taking license to speak straightforwardly about sexuality is often difficult for mothers because it's difficult for women in general. Even today much of female sexuality is depicted in demeaning, restrictive ways that are not at all authentic. Cultural critic and University of Michigan professor of communications Susan Douglas ironically calls our society one of "enlightened sexism."[26] Women have the appearance of respecting and being at ease with their sexuality, but this is mainly an illusion. Douglas refers to the explosion of popular reality shows that feature female sexuality only as a means of maliciously competing with other women to seduce men as indicative of this. These include *Next*, *The Bachelor*, *Joe Millionaire*, and *The Flavor of Love*.[27] As for our girls, she reports that according to a 2002 report of the Guttmacher Institute especially since 1995, "as the amount of sexual content in the media has increased, exposure to thorough and reliable sex education has decreased."[28] More than three decades after the second wave of feminism, genuine experiences of female sexuality are still underrepresented in the media. Understanding the position our mothers and grandmothers were in can help us appreciate the weight of our reluctance to be open. Simone de Beauvoir first pointed out in *The Second Sex* that a mother "projects upon her daughter all the ambiguities of her relation with herself."[29] Shame begets shame and ignorance begets ignorance. Fortunately, with each generation more and more sexism has been diluted, and, armed with much more information than our ancestors had, we contemporary mothers have the ability to exponentially hasten the process by forging new paths of honesty.

Being truthful with our daughters involves what we believe to be psychological risk. Will we do it wrong? Will we overwhelm them? Will we encourage them to be sexually active too soon? Will we lose their respect if we share aspects of our sexuality? We tend to devote so much time trying not to damage them in these ways that we often don't take into consideration the psychological risks of not being honest: creating distance between us; leaving them to be confused, ashamed, uneducated, and feeling unsupported in their erotic life, and driving our own sexuality further down. Being more honest and open with them will foster their authenticity as women as well as our own. Hiding our human sexuality is an inauthentic way to go through our lives.

With regard to understanding masturbation and its role in helping establish sexual authenticity and health, in reading all of these women's experiences, my mind repeatedly fell to English poet John Donne's sonnet popularly known as "Death Be Not Proud"[30]: "Death be not proud," the poem begins, "though some have called thee/Mighty and dreadful, for thou art not so." The speaker goes on to give Death a dressing-down, saying, you're nothing to fear, look at the terrible company you keep, you keep company with war and poison and sickness! There are women who may believe that masturbation, like death in the sonnet, is something to be dreaded, something sinful or perverted. But look at the company it keeps when we contemplate what all of these women have to teach us about how masturbation is a part of their lives. Their private confessions form a collective voice that can influence us to change our understanding of masturbation from a simple behavior we'd probably never given a lot of thought to, to something much fuller. They elevate it to an experience that keeps company with music and dreams, nurturance, vitality and love, and the will to recover.

All good. All good for men and women, and boys, but especially for our girls, because 20 years down the road, when some other woman is conducting her sexual research, I want her to look at her findings and see a *new* generation of women who feel no guilt whatsoever over their human right to their erotic vitality.

Chapter Four

The Lifelong Conversation with Our Daughters about Sexuality

Whe might realize our daughters need our support as they discover their sexuality, but how do we give it to them? Many mothers are unsure of how to proceed and nervous about saying the wrong thing, but the only way we can make conversations about sex more comfortable is to try to keep having them consistently and over time. Creating that comfort zone will involve several things. It will require setting a tone that respects both the individuality and privacy of both parties; relaxing in the knowledge that, as long as we stay aware, we'll have opportunities to nurture these conversations as they pop up again and again in the routine of our lives; and appreciating how these conversations will facilitate the growth of our sexual selves, not only as mothers and daughters but as women in the world together. While this growing ease we share won't always be able to prevent the potential upheaval of our daughters' sexual complications or pain—from things like endometriosis, infertility, or sexual betrayal, for instance—it will have the power to reduce the extent of the suffering, because it's harder to suffer alone. The proven reliability of the safe, ongoing dialogue between ourselves and our daughters will be something our daughters can always count on to help them feel as centered as possible, even in difficult times. From the naming of their body parts when they're little, to concerns of infidelity whether they come in high school or in their forties, to helping with hot flashes, the closeness this open-ended dialogue can inspire is emotionally incomparable.

One of the maternal concerns that runs through our relationships with our daughters is worrying what they'll think of us if we reveal our own sexual experiences. Being able to have a sense of control over what we disclose is important in maintaining our own comfort level, and we should be able to determine for ourselves where those boundaries are. That being said, we also have to take our daughters' needs into consideration when establishing them. General withholding to suit our own discomfort is the problem that lets down our daughters, not our judiciousness. In fact, one of the most important things we should teach our daughters about sexuality is that the personal boundary of privacy is one of the fabulous qualities that makes sexuality distinct from everything else.

But there's a difference between teaching our daughters privacy and keeping them in the dark about the nature of their sexuality because we're uncomfortable talking about it. One 19-year-old woman voices the problem and our dread when she says that she wouldn't teach her daughter about masturbation because she *wouldn't know how [to do so] without being a perv.* We as mothers need to examine our motivation at these decision-making junctures as we decide what we talk about and what we don't. If we remain silent simply because we won't challenge our own emotional status quo on behalf of our daughters, or because we're merely following the tracks laid down by our mothers, we aren't supporting our daughters but being complacent. We need to take into consideration the improved quality of life available to our girls—a quality of life that was unavailable to our mothers and grandmothers—and use this realization as a springboard to reflect on how we might relieve our daughters of some of the guilt we were raised to believe was endemic to our sexuality. As mothers, there is a huge distinction between our making a *conscious* decision not to teach our daughters and merely mimicking the "Don't Go There" messages our mothers gave us.

For our daughters, the importance of boundaries and privacy is that they allow them to learn from their own experience, and to test their own beliefs and moral compass. How they'll learn life lessons in the sexual arena will be incredibly similar to how they'll learn them in every other arena of their lives, and together all of these lessons will dovetail into a lived experience that will help them become more and more solid in their sense of themselves.

When my daughter was 12, we were talking about a routine school day and I was peppering her with questions on that epicenter of tween drama, the lunch table. When she'd had enough of my questions she threw me an impish smirk and said, "You know, you're getting a little all up in my business." In moments when she won't tolerate my nosiness I like to feign drama and say, "Oh, excuse me, Sister Mary Obstinate." But she's right to uphold her privacy. At the lunch table there will be issues she wants to, and should, resolve on her own, and others on which she may want my input. Her sexual growth should be no different. I want her to know I'm there for her when she needs me, but I also have to leave room for her to learn how to show up for herself.

There will be times our daughters won't want to include us in their pursuit of information, but there will be other times they'll bring us their questions. Sometimes they'll blurt them out and we won't even see them coming. In most areas of our lives we tend to fear the unexpected, but I think one of the most exciting aspects of parenting is never knowing when, where, or whom your kid is going to ask something that will take you by complete surprise and perhaps cause blushing or stammering on your part.

When my daughter was nine, my friend's father died after a long bout with illness, and because my daughter loves this friend, I took her to the memorial service with me. She had never experienced a death or seen a dead body before, and I wasn't sure how she would react as we entered the viewing room in the funeral home, so I hovered over her, constantly asking how she was feeling. We were standing in the back of the room and I asked her if she wanted to go up to the casket, or stay in the back, and she chose to sit with me on a settee against the side wall. I could see that she was deep in thought, so I whispered to her that if she had any questions she could ask me anything she wanted. She leaned into me and cupped her hand to my ear and whispered back, "How do you get a tampon out once it's in?" And I found myself saying something I'd never had cause to say at a memorial before. "There's a string, baby, and you pull it." It is, as you might imagine, my favorite funereal moment.

We think we're afraid of those surprise attack questions, but there's a good chance those are the ones we'll remember as some of the sweetest interactions we've ever had. Our run-ins with our daughters on sexual topics might come from our desire to teach them something, or they might come in response to a question they introduce. In either case, when they're young, something simple and straightforward is best. When they're older we'll be able to read how much they want to know based on the extent to which they choose to extend the conversation, regardless of who started it.

Once again using masturbation as the template for sexuality, we don't feel comfortable talking to our daughters about it in part because we don't want to be seen as perverts, but also because we're so afraid they'll wonder if we masturbate. If we begin the process of giving them information and a healthy sense about it when it will be of greatest benefit to them, up to age eight or nine, there's no cause for worry because their understanding of masturbation can only be presexual because they haven't the cognitive or physical basis for a more adult/sexual-as-we-know-it understanding. Their curiosity is very concrete, so our responses can be too. When they enter adolescence their curiosity will become more sexualized because their bodies are, but the relieving news at that age is that they'll wonder if we masturbate whether we teach them about it or not, and the reason they'll wonder won't be so much about us; it will be because they'll want to know if *they're* normal. They'll want to know if anyone else is doing it, and their curiosity will turn their brains into a teenage version of a Richard Scarry Busytown of others who might be doing what they've just discovered in a more sexual way. Does the mailman masturbate? The librarian? The hot guy who sat in front of them at the movie theater? The new girl in school? Us? We will not be the sole focus of their curiosity. In fact, teens will actually be spending a great deal of their mental effort wondering if we or anyone else knows *they're* doing it.

We need to remember what it was like when we first discovered physical sensations that felt tingly in a confusing and anxiety-provoking way. We can help our daughters feel comfortable in that exploration simply by sharing with them what it felt like when we were younger and equally bewildered and excited. We worry we'll be put in a position to give our daughters instructions on how to be sexual, to provide them with all of the "naughty" details, but that isn't what they need. They need straightforward information delivered without moral judgment, in age-appropriate doses. In addition to that, they need to feel our emotional presence in supporting their understanding of sexuality—theirs *and* ours—as a valued part of life.

AN AGE-APPROPRIATE GUIDE FOR DISCUSSING MASTURBATION AND SEXUALITY

Continuing to use masturbation as a learning tool to inform how we can rethink our maternal role in talking to our daughters about all aspects of sexuality, here is the list of what adult women in my study wish their mothers had taught them, which we can use as a guide. Women wished that they had known that masturbation is

- normal
- a way for me to get to know my own body
- a way for me to get to know my own sexuality and what I respond to
- a way for me to know what I like so I can let my partner know what turns me on

The following guidelines will help mothers become more confident sexual educators by providing an in-depth understanding of masturbation.

Birth–Age 3

Important mothering tasks at this age are:

1. Love her in all ways, including being physically affectionate and emotionally comforting.
2. Teach her the accurate names for all of her body parts without drawing moral distinctions between them.
3. Be conscious of the importance of physical connection and sensuality from the beginning of her infancy so that your comfort with its role in her life will grow right along with her.

I can't stress enough that the more basics you give her when she's really young, the easier it will be to add more and more information as she gets older, and the more confident you'll feel sharing it with her. Most of us begin teaching our babies and toddlers about their anatomy and physical sensation without even thinking about it. Games such as "This Little Piggy Went to Market" delight babies because they feel something good each time we squeeze one of their miniature toes, but its benefits go beyond that. Every time you play it you're also bonding in a sensual moment, and teaching her an appreciation and respect for her body *and* the pleasures of sharing it, even in her infancy. Being aware of this can help you make a smoother transition from the specialness of your baby sharing healthy physical pleasure with you to respecting the specialness of your young adult daughter's desire for more sexualized physical pleasure as she matures. The developmental needs of an infant and an adult are the same here: the need to connect to another through physical expression.

Again, teach her the correct terms for her body parts. When she's in the tub and asks you a question about her genitalia, like "What's this?" respond with an honest and accurate answer. It's not sexual to her yet; to her it's just another building block in understanding who she is as a small human being. For her, pointing to her vulva for its name is no different than pointing to the fleshy part of her ear and learning, "That's your earlobe."

You can also effortlessly slip in anatomy lessons by taking the opportunities she presents to you indirectly. If you notice when she's toilet training that she has a rash on her labia, you can point to it and say something like, "Is your labia sore? Do you want me to put some cream on it?" Or if she points to your breasts and asks what they are, you can answer, "Those are my breasts. You have them too." Again, no need to say any more than that. You're teaching her these are normal things that can be talked about. What you don't want to do at this stage is insert a negative moral message. If your daughter points to her clitoris and asks what it is and you ignore her, change the subject, or get anxious and say "Don't touch that" she'll learn it's the anatomical equivalent of a no-fly zone. She'll learn that whatever it is she just asked you about, it is *very* different from her earlobe, and not in a good way.

If you notice your daughter is rubbing herself, remember it's not sexual for her; she's doing it because it feels good and it's soothing her. She might tend to do it when she's sleepy, for instance, and it isn't something you need to comment on. But because our culture isn't very open with masturbation, as she gets older, if she's doing it in public in a way that makes you uncomfortable and you feel you have to say something, be mindful not to shame her. Show openness in your face. Smile and say something like, "I know that feels good, but it's private so it's better if you do it when you can have your privacy," or "I know that feels good, but it's private and special, so people don't do it in public."

If your daughter is doing it excessively it's probably because something has her wound up or upset and she's using it to comfort herself, so you might try to suss out what's upsetting her. But if she's touching herself in a way that feels sexually precocious to you; if she seems to have inappropriate knowledge or interest in things of a sexual nature; or if her behavior seems different around a particular person (afraid, avoidant, unusually quiet) these could be signs of sexual abuse that need to be taken seriously. This might be a time to check her underwear or pajamas for stains or tears in the fabric, and to investigate further. This holds true for older daughters as well.

The Preschool Years

Important mothering tasks for this age group are:

1. Be candid. Speak to your daughter or answer her questions truthfully and very simply.
2. Teach her masturbation is normal and special because it feels good but should be done in private.
3. Focus on what your daughter is learning and let your respect for that process temper any embarrassment you might feel.

These years tend to involve big change because kids are starting nursery school and kindergarten. Up to age four children's physical exploration is mainly about getting to know their own bodies. Around ages four or five you might see more curiosity about other people's bodies—yours and other children's. In these years your daughter's questions might become a little more specific, and the differences between girls and boys and women and men might be more intriguing to her. Behavior during this time might include more presexual genital touching. At home, you can continue to instill in her a sense of understanding and respectful privacy. But if she's exploring her own body by masturbating at school, for example, and you get a call from the teacher, or if she does it on a play date, and you get a call from the other parent, don't panic. Your daughter has done nothing other than behave like a member of the human race. Politely thank the teacher or parent for the information, and don't let them shame you. When your daughter comes home, you can have another conversation on how her genitals are private parts of her body and repeat that there's absolutely nothing wrong with touching them, but because it's a special, private thing she should do it in her alone time. This isn't to teach prudishness. It's to help our children establish the boundaries between private and public, boundaries they'll need to use throughout their lives. We really don't want to raise a generation of children who become adults that masturbate next to you at Starbucks because they're antsy waiting in line for their venti lattes. When she's in her teenage years you can teach her that masturbation can also take place during partnered sex, which will somewhat expand the definition of private.

If your daughter is exploring someone else's body, it might be through an activity such as playing doctor. This is standard fare. Preschool-age children still don't have the emotional or cognitive capacity to experience such activities as adults would. She might also take herself on verbal fact-finding missions with her friends, like the comparative analysis on the shape and color of their mothers' pubic hair that one of my friends overheard taking place one day between a group of kindergarten girls that included our daughters.

Remember, even if it makes *you* blush, your daughter won't know it's blush-worthy. Instead of getting stuck in your own embarrassment or panic, try to be open to feeling excited for your daughter, who's beginning to sort out who she is in the context of others. Sorting out sexuality is a huge lifelong developmental quest. *I'm* still sorting it out. Be happy that you're there watching her come into her own in this fundamental way, and be proud that you're giving her not only the words and the visuals for it but setting a tone of acceptance.

The following story actually comes not from a mother but from a father, and while a focus on fathers is fodder for another book, I'm going to tell it because it's hysterical and, to my mind, incredibly sweet.

One of my closest friends was cooking dinner for his five-year-old daughter when his wife was out of town on business. His daughter had just gotten out of the tub, and she walked into the kitchen in her jammies with a smile on her face, holding her index finger up to his nose as she approached him. Because she was smiling, he was smiling back and bending down toward her as she said, "My vagina smells pretty, Daddy!" her finger held high so he too might enjoy the pretty smell.

Her father, face now frozen in a state of shock, kept smiling, his eyes wide as saucers, thinking, "Oh-my-god-what-do-I-do-what-do-I-do-what-do-I-do!!!?" He was so taken aback he couldn't think of a single thing to say, so he just kept smiling, nodded his head, and said, "Mmm-hmmm!" She beamed back at him and toddled off, and as soon as she was out of the room he resumed breathing.

Her mother had set the stage for all of this to happen. She'd taught her daughter the names of her body parts and then she let these anatomy lessons progress naturally. We all know children can log in hours exploring the interiors of their nostrils, and they will explore whatever their little hands can reach. Her mother didn't do anything to inhibit this exploration, so the little girl didn't attach anything negative to this delightfully quirky announcement she wanted to make to her father.

The daughter probably won't even remember this incident because her father mirrored her delight and it was to her just another nice interchange that day, like bringing home a painting from school and having him hang it on the refrigerator. What makes this story perfect is the absence of the father doing something to make it memorable for her in a shaming way. Even in a panic, he instinctively sensed the right thing to do was to recognize she was showing him something she was proud of. She toddled off feeling happy because her father had validated her reality. Her vagina smelled pretty and her father was pleased for her. That's the five-year-old's experience. It was about her sexual anatomy, but there was nothing sexual or inappropriate, it was all presexual in her understanding. If the other messages she gets from her parents are similarly positive, if we fast-forward 30 years she will likely have gone from a little girl who "knows" her vagina smells pretty to a woman who "knows" her vagina smells pretty. She probably won't connect it to that evening in the kitchen; she'll simply experience it as a part of who she is, and she'll expect no different a reaction from her sexual partners. It will be a mark of her comfort and confidence, and she won't ever feel she has to choose between the love and respect of her father and her right to her sexuality.

Elementary Age

Important tasks of the mother at this age are:

1. Continue to speak and answer truthfully, but move it up a notch from being very simple, to simple.

2. When she's eight or nine, buy her Robie H. Harris and Michael Emberley's *It's Perfectly Normal: Changing Bodies, Growing Up, Sex and Sexual Health* ($10.99).

3. Be open to the ways you can mother yourself as you mother her. The more connected to you she feels in learning about her body, the less alienated from herself she'll be. And the same can be true for you. She'll be beginning the process of positively assimilating her sexuality into the whole of who she is, and you'll be furthering your own assimilation as you experience looking at your sexuality through the eyes of a mother raising a girl.

This age period is known as the latency phase in Freud's psychosexual stages of development. I like to think of it as the emotional, psychological, and physical vacation children need before puberty begins to rock their world. (And ours.) This is the time to cram in as much information as you see fit because you've already given her the rudiments, so she's ready for more, and because her body hasn't begun to change she's not scared by sexual information yet. It's also a fun time. At this age she's totally excited by what's in store for her, but when adolescence starts to set in talking about sex becomes frightening or more overwhelming because then it's for real—by then it's going on inside her body and she witnesses it in her friends. My daughter was totally chatty, open, and eager to ask questions or listen to what I wanted to teach her when she was in elementary school. At 13, she turned into a clam.

The mid to late-elementary years are a fabulous time to bring in books, tampons, bras—whatever she seems curious about. Your daughter may always have been around your feminine hygiene products, but now she might want to unwrap them and check them out with a deeper understanding of their function and their upcoming relation to her body. Often when my daughter had girlfriends over during these years, I'd notice my bra drawer would be askew, my high heels would go missing, and there would be little fingerprints in my concealer. They started to play dress-up in a more sophisticated way, wanting to look and feel like grown-up women, and I'd have a constant flow of girls rummaging through my closet to pick out their favorite items. Their excitement was infectious, and it made me reflect on my own girlhood and appreciate my adult sexuality anew. Also, be aware that there are many, many ways to look like a grown woman. If you find your daughter isn't into traditionally female things, or if she prefers to dress up in men's clothing, celebrate her. Our girls need to be free to grow into their sexual identities feeling the full force of our love behind them.

Educational books written for children are a great way to help young daughters develop an understanding of sexuality at this age. I recommend *It's Perfectly Normal*—a watercolor-illustrated, comprehensive guide written in language that's child-friendly—not so you can take the backseat to a book in educating your daughter, but because it will provide you with visual aids that will make it easier for your daughter to absorb the learning. Because it's laid out to reflect the line of children's development, you can go through it bit by bit over the years, reading only the chapters that feel right for your daughter at any given time. Since age eight is the time you should start preparing her for her first period, this book can be a companion for both of you to enjoy to cover all the bases. Another of its greatest assets is the chapter on homosexuality. It can provide an opportunity for you to be sure you make room for her right to respond to arousal the way her body will feel it, whether it's directed toward males or females. The reality is that you won't know your daughter's sexual orientation unless or until she tells you, and beginning this discussion at this age will let her know that, above all, you want her to follow her body and heart so she'll be happy and true to herself throughout her life.

The most important thing here is to read the book *with* her so she feels your support and openness. Then, she can ask you questions as you go, and you can measure her reactions to things and learn more about her. Do it in bed with a bowl of popcorn. If, for some reason, she's totally against reading it with you, don't force it. Give her her space. But check in with her from time to time to see if she might feel ready in the future.

Middle School

Important mothering tasks for this age are:

1. Speak to your daughter and answer her questions truthfully with more complexity.

2. Respect the reality that who she is in the world now begins to develop and expand to include more adult sexual feeling and meaning.

3. Remember what it was like for you when your body began to change and you were neither a little girl nor a young woman. Remember how it felt to stand on shifting sand, day in and day out.

4. Share stories of your own experience at her age, ones that will help her see herself on a plane of females who all went through something similar.

In these years your daughter's body will be changing so fast, much of her energy will be devoted to just holding it together physically, socially, and sexually, and she'll look to her peer group for a healthy sense of belonging that will enable her to become increasingly independent.

This isn't a time to be intrusive. You don't want to ask her if she's masturbating, for example. Your job was to teach her it's OK, and you've already done that. Now is the time to let her self-discovery kick in, in a new way, and to show her that you respect her need for privacy. But she is ready for more complex information, and you can update her understanding of things from the last time you discussed them. From late middle school into early high school you can give her increasingly more sophisticated material. This is a great time to start taking advantage of sexual content you'll stumble upon together through lyrics, television, movies, or conversations with others, because discussing it as it informally pops up may be less embarrassing for her than it would be through something more akin to a lecture. For example, if you read about masturbation in *It's Perfectly Normal* with your daughter when she was ten, and then a couple of years later you're watching a movie and there's a reference to masturbation, you can pick up the lesson by discussing its meaning within the context of the story line. The simplest way to start that conversation is to say, "Do you know what they're talking about? They're talking about masturbation." And take it from there.

If your worst nightmare comes true and she flat out asks you if you masturbate (which she probably won't do), you can answer, "Almost everyone—if not everyone—does. For me it's very private and I prefer to keep it that way, but I want you to know it's normal and I don't ever want you to feel guilty about it. It's a way to get to know yourself, and to understand and enjoy your body and your own sexuality." Even if she leaves the room saying, "Eeww!" you'll have taught her: (1) that sexuality, including masturbation, is normal and healthy; (2) that you're a sexual creature just as she is, so she won't have to fear losing your love, respect, or understanding if she follows her sexual nature; (3) that she too can protect her privacy when it comes to making decisions about what she discloses of her intimate life; and (4) that even though she'll have to learn through her own unique experiences, she won't have to learn, as many of us before her had to, in taboo-laden isolation.

You can share stories of your first period with her at this age, or what it felt like to, seemingly overnight, have underarm and pubic hair. Extend to her your memories to let her know she's not alone, and that the changes she's going through can be talked about. It's the emotional piece of the sharing we need to celebrate because that's where the sense of belonging will come from.

Our daughters should learn about sexuality within their peer group, just not exclusively. We often outsource our daughters' sexual education just like financial and tech companies outsource customer service to India. Not being given access to information on their sexuality from women who love them causes girls to search elsewhere, in places into which female sexuality has been displaced in an effort to be expressed somewhere...anywhere. They'll be forced to learn from other models: from cartoonish and misogynist representations of women in music videos, or advertisements in which women are orgasming on the ground over their new handbags.

They'll come to learn through observation over the years that "real" women can express their sexuality only through the smaller victories of erotic pleasure such as finding it quite normal that women in restaurants or at the Thanksgiving table will openly tilt their heads back, close their eyes, and moan unabashedly...over a piece of chocolate...with the full support and understanding of all onlookers.

Late middle school is also the perfect time for you to start to balance the bits of information and misinformation your daughter's getting in her peer group as well as what she gets in health class. And God only knows what our kids will access on the internet. You are your daughter's primary source for accurate information, and her peer group is her primary source for processing it. Don't just hand her off to the health teacher or school nurse. This is a stance supported by the American Academy of Child and Adolescent Psychiatry: "Talking to your children about love, intimacy and sex is an important part of parenting....Children and adolescents need input and guidance from parents to help them make healthy and appropriate decisions regarding their sexual behavior since they can be confused and over stimulated by what they see and hear."[1] Remember, the information we give our daughters builds a strong knowledge base, but our ongoing dialogue with them builds emotional stability and trust.

This middle school stage can be anxiety provoking for mothers because our daughters now do have the capacity to start processing sexual material on a more sexual level. And some girls become sexually active at this age. Even if they're engaging in sexual behavior, their understanding of it can only be incredibly narrow because they haven't had a range of lived experience with which to put it into context. Keep in mind this is the age when kids need to pretend they have a more sophisticated knowledge than they actually do of the terminology and behaviors.

On that note, let's move from the solitary nature of masturbation to the more interpersonal realm that tends to frighten parents even more. Let's take, for instance, oral sex. Remember when you didn't know what oral sex was? Remember when you wouldn't have dared to ask an adult what a blow job was, and were too afraid of being cast out by your friends as stupid if you admitted you didn't know (even though they probably didn't know either)? Use your memories of those feelings to motivate yourself to talk to your daughter. Then fast-forward to where you are now. Whether you are a woman who enjoys oral sex or a woman who's uncomfortable with it, you can reach out to your daughter from either position and support *her* comfort in learning about it. And be clear with yourself: educating her is a way of preparing her for the process of understanding her ability to determine for herself whether and when she feels ready for it. Educating her does not mean you feel she is ready for oral sex. Once again, you have to pull back your fears enough to see that you're preparing her for this just like you prepared her for walking. When she was six months old you didn't shove her away from you one day hoping she'd walk. It was a long process that began with letting her wrap her fingers around yours while you walked together with her between your knees teetering side to side like a metronome. Sexuality is the same. How will our daughters go from being girls who might want to know the definition of a sexual word to women who, say, find their own meaning and use of oral sex in their lives? I believe they should know we are happy to be there whenever they need us throughout that journey. I've heard stories of mothers harming their daughters by not having appropriate sexual boundaries (like having loud sex with a series of different boyfriends, with the bedroom door open), or by overwhelming their daughters with sexual content (like sharing inappropriately explicit details of their sex lives). But I have never heard a daughter complain that her mother gave her appropriate information too early. I've only heard the opposite, of daughters' disappointment that they got no information whatsoever, or too little too late. In the past mothers have been so afraid of broaching sexual topics with their daughters that they wait and wait until they look back and realize they were so complacent in their waiting that they missed the timeliest of opportunities.

Search your own memories and try to remember all you didn't know. There are simple things you can help her with, like the first time she hears the term "blow job," when she'll likely, as we all did at first, think it must surely involve some blowing. You can leave her to her peer group, the blind leading the blind, or you can spare her some of her embarrassment and confusion by giving her the facts. And, now because she's old enough, you can also throw in some concepts that are probably important to you. You can teach her that oral sex is when one person puts their mouth on another person's genitals, and that a blow job is slang for oral sex when it's performed on a penis. Then you can relax and think to yourself: "There. I did it." Next, since you're there already, you can glide right into defining cunnilingus and giving her the laundry list of oral sex synonyms so she'll have an accurate understanding of all of them, thereby rescuing her from any of their residual fear and confusion—because just as there is no actual blowing, she might be relieved to know there is no actual eating, and so on. You also must tell her that it is possible for HIV and STDs to be transmitted through oral sex. She'll probably be embarrassed throughout this conversation, but that's to be expected and doesn't mean the information isn't useful to her.

You can tell her you know it's embarrassing, but you want her to have correct information on sexual matters and for her to know the door is always open for the two of you to talk about them. You can stop there and pick up the thread again later when you can personalize this conversation further and share your hopes for how she might come to know oral sex as a woman. Now is your chance to weigh in against oral sex as a brief encounter taken out of the context of a relationship, and to make sure you vote against it solely as a means to win someone's affections. You can tell her it's something you really want her to wait for because when she does have it you want her to feel ready and comfortable with that level of intimacy, and you can be sure to instill an appreciation for the mutuality of all intimacy by teaching her that healthy intimacy is a two-way street of giving *and receiving*. Lastly, make sure, sometime in late-middle school to early-high school, that you extend your anatomy lesson to include orgasm and the different levels of sensitivity in the clitoris and vagina. Let her know not all women climax from vaginal stimulation and that she should feel comfortable learning the unique responses of her own body. And if this makes you nervous, comfort yourself with the knowledge that the more she owns her own sexuality the less she'll have to rely on partnered sex as the only means by which she can experience it.

Be aware that as she gets older, her understanding of the intimate nature of what she wants to know about will likely make her more self-conscious about asking you questions, and while you don't want to inundate her with information, you don't always want the burden to fall on her to ask you things. If she does come to you with questions, answer them directly, and if this unnerves you, try to temper your reaction by remembering she wouldn't be asking you if she didn't want to know. At each of these moments, try to be clear that she's presenting you with a choice: you can be there for her in the way she needs you, or you can let her down and create awkwardness in her and in your relationship. You can also bolster your resolve to be there for her by understanding that if she doesn't learn from you, she'll learn from someone else.

High School

Important mothering tasks at this age are:

1. Start to build a more complex bridge between ideas and concepts— such as the bridge from the idea of sex to the concepts of intimacy and erotic longing.
2. Advocate waiting for sexual activity by teaching your daughter that the longer she waits, the more comfortable she'll be.
3. Teach her that you share and value the part of desire and sensuality that's so compelling it has the power to change our rate of breathing.
4. Trace the difference in your own sex life from the time you lost your virginity to now, and recognize that it was through practicing and learning that you arrived where you are.

In the early high school years your message to your daughter should be: You might be having a hard time with me but I am here for you. Your daughter will probably see you as an embarrassment. As a friend who is also a child psychologist says, during this period it can be like trying to love a porcupine. They're prickly. Their hormones are in disarray and they desperately need to forsake you to immerse themselves in their peer group and develop identities outside the family in preparation for later separation into adulthood.

You've taught her the essentials, and now she needs your support in stringing them together to form concepts. How does a daughter go from the private safety of masturbation to complexities of intimacy with another person, for example? Let's face it, these are quandaries adult women face, so of course it's daunting for our daughters. How does she go from having this new body to figuring out how to live in it? It's your job to be there when she needs you for support, questions, advice, and limit setting so she feels safe. This is the time she'll want to go out on her own to learn more about herself, and because she knows you're there for her (even if she doesn't want to be seen in public with you) it will be easier for her to turn to you when she needs you. Daughters at this age have a lot of information cognitively but they haven't assimilated it experientially and emotionally. Later in high school, around age 16, it tends to come together. Their periods have calmed down a bit, they're realizing the seriousness of school, not rebelling so much, and maybe settling into a relationship and a calmer place with parents. Over the ages of 16–19 an emancipation from some of the turmoil occurs as young women's personalities and sexuality become more assimilated.

Again, you don't want to intrude on your daughter's privacy, but whether it's broached directly or indirectly, you can teach her that masturbation is a healthy way for teens to experience stress release, self-soothing, and to quell desire. It is by far the healthier alternative to other more destructive ways teens cope, like engaging in stress eating, purging, self-mutilation, promiscuous sex, or consuming alcohol or drugs. Even if your discussions remain open, you can also recommend she refer to the website Scarleteen. com for any information she wants to seek on her own. Its content is direct, and compiled for teens and young adults based on what they want to know.

And when discussing masturbation in the context of safe sex practices, do it not from a place of fear but as an extension of what your responsibility to her has been since she was born: to help her keep safe because you love her. You don't want to inadvertently help her to equate erotic longing with fear of pregnancy and infection. The freedom to long and the responsibility to protect are two separate issues of sexuality, and our society's denial of female desire, especially in girls, is already enough for them to contend with without our unconsciously adding to it. Of her interviews on desire with teenage girls Nathalie Bartle, a professor at Drexel University's School of Public Health, writes, "Our failure to discuss female sexual desire further disempowers our girls. It takes no stretch of the imagination to understand how a young woman who feels desire but whose feelings are not legitimized or discussed either at home or in school may feel cautious, and perhaps ashamed, about her own natural longings."[2] Desire is not what causes pregnancy and infection.

Witnessing this time in your daughter's life also gives you a chance to look over your own sexual rites of passage and be respectful of them. Even if you have regrets or wish you'd done something differently, you have to respect the fact that, at that time, you were doing your best in beginning to learn how to live within your sexuality *and* within the mind-boggling world of relationships. Even if you remained a virgin through high school, you were still absorbing and learning. Remember that we learn through observation, and by making mistakes as well as by doing something well. One of my favorite quotes is from U.S. astronaut Edwin "Buzz" Aldrin, who said in an *Esquire* interview, "The final frontier may be human relationships, one person to another."[3] For him, walking on the moon was easier to navigate than understanding human relationships. If nonsexual relationships are complex to navigate, sexual ones are that much more mysterious—maybe even more mysterious than astrophysics.

Now it's time to afford your daughter the same opportunity to explore these mysteries of desire. The difference for her will hopefully be that, unlike generations before her, she won't have to learn in a lonely vacuum.

Because you have always spoken to her about female sexuality, she will have choices. When she chooses to learn on her own without you, she'll be choosing to protect her privacy. When she wants to have you with her, she'll be choosing you because she knows you'll be there and you've proven she can rely on you.

Don't let your fears get in the way of seeing what she might need. If she wants your counsel on handling more mature relationships, you should be proud that you've raised her to feel comfortable approaching you. If you lost your virginity in high school and you believe your daughter's considering losing hers at the same age you were, but you want her to wait, be prepared for her to ask you when you had your first experience, and give it some thought. Respect the fact that however you arrived at it, when you were her age you did make the decision to have sex. Now she could be at that decision-making point. This is where a lot of mothers would bail and never face the issue, and still others would try to scare their daughters out of it. If it makes you feel any better, I know from the loss of virginity questionnaire that respondents completed that many of the women in my study didn't attach that much emotional memory to how and when they lost their virginity. In fact, a lot of women reported just being glad it was over, and saw it more as the beginning of a sex life than a huge pivotal moment.

The most important thing is to have a conversation so you can teach your daughter how to weigh her options and her feelings at all important junctures. Don't lecture. Listen and talk.

In England, Hogarth and Ingham found in their study on masturbation and sexual health that the group of girls with the healthiest attitudes toward masturbation had open communication with their mothers. These girls were able to experience pleasure, and to speak about it without embarrassment. They described an appreciation of their mothers' sharing of their own experiences, confusion, and pressures with regard to sexuality, and valued that their mothers set a reciprocal conversational tone around sexual matters, talking with them, not at them. The authors also found that being talked at was a common complaint registered by the girls who were less sexually comfortable.[4]

Let your daughter use conversations with you both to explore her options and to firm up her own perspectives. If you wish you had waited longer before you had sex, tell her that, and give her your reasons; if you felt fine with the age at which you lost your virginity, tell her that. The goal is to not make her feel she has to choose between following the inclinations of her body and disappointing you. Your role is to be an adviser and to help her find her own way of growing into her sexuality.

It's also helpful to let your daughter bear witness to you when you're feeling sexy or sexual. Comment on it, and celebrate it. You don't even have to be in a sexual relationship to have such feelings. It could be as simple as saying, "I always feel sexy when I wear this shirt," or when relating a love story of yours being sure to include how you felt in your own body—and use any language you feel comfortable with. You can say you felt on fire, you can say you were given the vapors. It doesn't matter. She just needs to know it's there in you and that it makes you feel alive. Don't be complicit in contributing to the stereotype that mothers aren't sexual.

Whether you're straight, gay, or bi, and whether she's straight, gay, or bi, it's about being there for your daughter in ways you wish your mother had been there for you. It doesn't matter if you were a virgin until you were 30, or the most promiscuous girl in your hometown; your task is to uphold a sense of mutual respect. As you help your daughter develop and protect her integrity, you'll be doing the same for yourself. This is a time to cultivate conversations that show her you value her sexual well-being as well as your own.

INTRODUCING THE SUBJECT IF YOUR DAUGHTER IS OLDER AND YOU'VE NEVER TALKED ABOUT SEXUALITY

I abide by the admonition of that great Nike ad campaign. Just do it. Don't wait for the perfect time. You can tell her you feel awkward bringing it up, but you're doing it because how she feels is important to you. You can even use this book. You can tell her you recently read something that said women still feel guilty about masturbation, and that even though you've never spoken about it with her before, you want her to know that you would never want her to feel guilty about any part of her sexuality. You can tell her you never talked to her about it before because you weren't raised to feel comfortable doing so. And if you want to, you can tell her you're sorry if you did anything that might have contributed to her feeling guilt or shame, and let her know you only wish for her happiness. As a therapist who works with women well into middle age, I can assure you your daughter could be in her sixties and still benefit from hearing you say that.

Modern Mothering

Chapter Five

What Do You Most Want to Know about Your Mother but Would Never Ask?

Q: What do you most want to know about your mother but would never ask, and what keeps you from asking?

A: Why she talked so much about being a virgin before she got married. [I don't ask because] she will lie.

W e live in a culture that encourages women to withhold information about our erotic lives from everyone, including immediate family, for propriety's sake. This is especially true for mothers. It's done by creating a false image of a woman who, when she becomes a mother, gives herself over entirely to nurturing. No matter how sexually alive she was before, as soon as she becomes a mother we act as though her erotic life is over.

Society insists on seeing us as asexual, and considers the act of revealing sexual information to our adult daughters to be like the divulging of some threatening, deeply held secrets found in Gothic novels. But while society might want us to lock our sexual past away, our daughters do not. Grown daughters in my study—from their twenties through middle age— yearn to know how our sexuality informed us as women when we were at the most formative turning points of our lives. They make it touchingly clear that they're curious about this because they want to understand us as women, and let that understanding flow over them to inform how they see themselves in their own lives. Our daughters want to comprehend our sexuality, past and present, to put us in the context of the women we are today; and they want to use this knowledge to contextualize how they live with their own sexuality and desire.

A daughter's measurement of her life against her mother's is one of the most comprehensive influences on her development as a woman. And as our daughters become adults we continue to influence their development. They wonder about our mature love relationships as they evaluate their own, and they watch us even when we don't know it. They see what we respond to with joy, and what elicits feelings of misery, and then they draw conclusions about how those things might be achieved or avoided in their own lives. They use this information to judge whether they want to be like us, or whether they need to go in a different direction to be happy. It is a natural process of getting to know their own identity as they grapple with who they are. Much of what our daughters need to measure against us is fairly apparent and readily accessible to them. They experience through our interactions with them how we feel about mothering, or they read our moods when we come home from work and listen to the way we talk about it, they observe us with our friends, and so on. But since we're trained to hide our sexuality, they're at a loss as to how to measure what it means to us and what it might mean for them. Because of its private nature, of course we don't model our intimate sexual behavior for them. But there is more to sexuality than sexual behavior—for example, the way it influences the general quality of our partnerships, and by extension, the health of our family life. The absence of these types of conversations in our relationships with our daughters makes our sexual narratives unavailable for their emotional use, which forces an unhealthy wedge between us. A crucial component of who we are as women is sealed off from one another. As was the case in their youth, because we hide our sexuality from our daughters, we teach them to hide it too, and often huge life issues with tremendous meaning are never given the respect and attention they deserve. Our adult daughters want to know if we can understand or have ever felt what they feel about major parts of living; and they wonder if they can risk finding out—like the daughter who wonders if her mother *ever questioned her sexuality [and doesn't ask] because then she' d know I'm questioning mine.*

The secrets we keep about our sexual existence leave our daughters longing to know more. Almost 50 percent of the women who responded to this question in the relationship with your mother questionnaire wanted to understand the depth of who we are as women in this regard, and here's a sampling of what they had to say.

WHAT DAUGHTERS WANT TO KNOW ABOUT THEIR MOTHERS BUT WON'T ASK

Hmm... was she really as innocent growing up as she says?

*   *   *

Why she stayed with my father.

*   *   *

If she's a closet lesbian.

*   *   *

A long-term marriage...how to do it.

*   *   *

Was she happy in her marriage? Satisfied and fulfilled—emotionally and sexually?

*   *   *

If she could do it over again, would she choose her current husband? Does she honestly feel compatible with him? Where would she rather be right now?

*   *   *

I want to know about her desire for sex; curious about her relationship choice with my father.

*   *   *

Who raped her.

* * *

From what little I know about it, to distill it to its simplest explanation, my parents divorced because Dad liked sex and Mom hated it, and this made them both miserable and led to other deal-breaking events. I've suspected for quite some time that she may have been abused or raped in her youth, because it would explain so many things about her. This is a question I don't think I could ever ask her.

* * *

Did she ever love my father?

* * *

If she ever regretted just being a housewife and mother when she had talent as a writer and artist. If she regretted staying with my father, her teenage sweetheart, for her whole adult life. If she regretted not getting much experience in the "big bad world."

* * *

Why she never told us about my oldest brother's birth and how she married my dad after he was born...why she was so ashamed.

* * *

I would like to ask my mother: Why didn't you date other men? Why did you allow Grandma to push you into a marriage you weren't sure was right?

* * *

Why she never had an affair after my father became ill.

* * *

Why doesn't she get help for her marriage, for her self-esteem issues?

* * *

Why must she play the victim role?

* * *

If she has a boyfriend.

* * *

I suspect that she had an abortion during my teenage years and I want to know for sure.

* * *

Did she ever find the love she should have had from my father?

* * *

How she deals with the painful body memory of rape. She was raped as an 18-year-old. That is how she lost her virginity. I wish I could kick that man in the balls.

* * *

If she had sex before she was married. If she's ever loved anyone as much as she loves my dad.

* * *

That I think she's had an affair.

* * *

I just recently asked her about her affair. I would find out more about that stage in her life. Did she leave my dad because she loved [her lover] so much, or did she just have to leave?

* * *

Did she have an affair?

* * *

Did putting up with my father make her happy?

* * *

Who is my father?

Each of these questions reveals a woman in search of the fundamentals not only of her mother, but of herself. They are of substantial psychological weight. Who is my mother as a woman? Who am I as a woman? And how does love work? These are the sorts of questions that have occupied women in my practice throughout my career; they are the questions my girlfriends and I are curious about, and they will be the ones that will challenge our daughters as they mature.

WHAT KEEPS THEM FROM ASKING?

Fear. I don't want to inspire disquiet.

* * *

Her homophobia and dishonesty.

* * *

I don't think she'd tell me if she was.

* * *

I don't want to make her feel bad—more than she already may feel about it.

* * *

She would get angry with me.

* * *

She will lie.

* * *

She'd never tell me the truth anyway.

* * *

Hurting her.

* * *

We can't even talk about sex in a positive way, not even about normal happy sex, not even about totally sanctioned-by-"God" married sex. I could never ask her about if she had been raped or molested. Because if it's true, it is her deepest darkest secret that probably no one on earth knows about.

* * *

I have asked her before and her answer was not an answer so much as a brush-off. I won't ask again, [because] it feels like an invasion of privacy.

* * *

THAT SHE WILL NEVER ANSWER!

* * *

She is incapable of answering questions like that. I've tried. I wouldn't trust her recollection anyway.

* * *

I am definitely not comfortable enough with her to ask that.

* * *

She will make me feel bad for asking.

The reasons our daughters don't ask us these questions are also of substantial psychological weight. They uncover a big problem. When it comes to sexuality, our daughters do not have faith in our ability to help them understand who we are, who they are, and how love works. Because of this, a crucial component of mothering lies dormant.

My client Alex's story can help us understand how these unasked and unanswered questions get played out in a daughter's life. When Alex was in her mid thirties she came to see me for treatment following a poor performance review in her job with a nonprofit foundation. Her work over the previous several years had been excellent, but in the last year she had become depressed and was having trouble focusing on projects to their completion. She had been with her husband for about seven years and told me, "The reason I'm completely distracted at work is because I'm afraid my marriage is going down the tubes. I love him, but I've fallen out of love with him. I don't want to sleep with him anymore, I'm wracked with guilt, and I don't know what to do or who to turn to. I need to get a handle on this because I can't afford to lose my job."

Alex described feeling alone at this impasse. Her husband was extremely uncomfortable talking about their problems, and in order to avoid difficult discussions he spent less and less time at home. They hadn't had sex for over a year, and in addition to retreating from her husband, she found herself falling out of touch with friends and family. She was embarrassed to confide in her girlfriends because she felt like a failure. When I asked, "Why a failure?" she said, "Because maybe they'll think I'm not working hard enough."

"Have you heard your friends say that about other couples going through difficulties?"

"No, but it's still my fear."

When I went on to ask if she had confided her feelings to her mother, Alex told me that although they had a very close relationship, "I can't tell her this stuff. I wish I could, but she won't talk about sex under any circumstances. I sometimes think my parents had sex once to conceive me and that was it. Besides, she hasn't seemed all that happy with my father and she stuck it out, so who am I to complain?"

"Would you have seen your mother as a failure if she hadn't stuck it out?"

"No! Of course not."

"Why not?"

"Because she's an incredible woman. They're both incredible."

"Are you concerned she would see you as a failure if your marriage ends?"

Alex paused, and then answered "She doesn't talk about these things, so I honestly don't know...but I worry about it."

The crisis in Alex's marriage was at the center of her concerns; and she came for therapy because being overwhelmed with that crisis had created a second one at work. The fragility of her marriage would have been enough to worry about, but in addition to that, she had other emotional baggage to carry. Much of the isolation, guilt, and shame she felt while worrying about being a failure was related to her observations regarding her mother's marriage. Even though her mother hadn't given her a firsthand account of why she was unhappy, Alex understood her mother had chosen to remain in her marriage despite her unhappiness and, from Alex's perspective, despite the absence of erotic love. Alex confided that not wanting to settle for a sexless marriage made her feel greedy—like she was hoping for too much and was ungrateful for what she had. In our work together she wondered whether her mother would have been happier without her father, or if she felt she made the right choice in staying with him. Alex also explored her consideration of leaving her husband as it compared to her mother's decision to stay. What influenced her mother in that direction? Love? Fear of change? Financial security, religious beliefs, or wanting to keep the family intact? Since her mother wouldn't disclose her motivation, all Alex could do was speculate. In this light, we discussed how both she and her mother probably faced the same quandary—how much is enough to stay in a marriage? We also determined that that is a question each woman has to answer for herself.

THE MOTHER-DAUGHTER DILEMMA

Why do we as mothers tend to keep our sexual narratives stowed away? We are inhibited about revealing them for multiple reasons. Not only because of our sense of propriety and because we believe it's easier to keep them private, but because we fear the penalties of being judged by our daughters as women who can't control our libidos, women without ethics, and women who've made mistakes. Even worse, we worry we will be judged as bad people. We feel our sexual integrity and moral standing—as well as that of our daughters—is at stake. In short, we project onto ourselves and our daughters that which society projects onto us.

We want our daughters to have as carefree a life as possible so we hold back on introducing them to the full complexities of sexuality in the illusion that if we don't speak of them, our daughters won't encounter them—in themselves *or* in us. But we ignore the penalty incurred by hiding the realities of our sexuality from them: Our daughters don't trust us to tell them the truth. That is a high price for us to pay for our shame. But even higher is the price our daughters pay when their mistrust of us gets transformed into a mistrust of themselves. When this is the case, as it often is, our adult daughters experience this mistrust through the stressful second-guessing of life-altering decisions they need to make as well as an undermining of their emotional beliefs about what is right and wrong for them. Can they be forthright about being in love? Can they determine for themselves when a relationship isn't fulfilling? Are they ready to take on the responsibility of parenting? Can they disclose if they were raped? Their mistrust interferes with an ability to read themselves and to act on their own behalf with confidence and integrity. As I see in my practice, rather than steering their own true course they get distracted by a focus on how they'll be judged by others. This is why Alex experienced her isolation, guilt, and shame.

Our daughters know that we guard the sexual narratives of our lives fiercely. I see the impediments to disclosing our sexual narratives to them as symptomatic of three things: (1) It's difficult to negotiate issues of privacy with anyone under any circumstances because the second we consider keeping something private, we understand disclosing it comes with the risk of judgment; (2) women have little historical reference for this kind of exchange because our mothers never talked to us about it; and (3) women are up against seemingly intractable sexism in a society that segments us into clearly delineated qualities of existence that preclude us from being seen as cohesive. Neither mothers nor daughters are seen as sexual creatures who desire.

Consequently, we fail to capitalize on the possibility that our daughters might want to know us in these ways. As mothers we undergo life-altering experiences within our sexual relationships, or sometimes another's violation of our sexuality, then cast these experiences off into a Sexual Bermuda Triangle. We keep all the information we've gained out of reach of our daughters who then have to find their own way through some of the very same challenges we faced without benefit of our experience. Every mother and daughter is entitled to her privacy, and it's important for each of them to determine for herself her comfort zones and how to safeguard them, especially around sexual trauma. But as with menstruation and masturbation, my concern is that mothers hold these things inside simply because we are repeating the behavior of our own mothers. Having had little support, it seems we find it just as difficult to reveal the sexual side of our lives to our daughters as generations before us did.

But as we have seen in the present text, it isn't only the bolder issues like infidelity and abortion that we're afraid to disclose. Even matters of our own arousal, such as never having had an orgasm, or matters of simple hygiene, like carrying tampons, cause us to anticipate the judgment of others. Based on this unfairness it's understandable we would be leery of disclosure. But unfortunately our fear of being shamed can blind us to what our daughters might want to know. And when our daughters sense and inherit our shame around these issues, as I frequently hear from women in my practice, they end up keeping the very same secrets from us, for fear of being judged. We become locked in a cycle of unwarranted disgrace. Mothers keep secrets from their daughters to save face, and daughters keep secrets from their mothers for the same reason, so round and round we go.

Because of that block between mothers and daughters, adult daughters are left to wrestle with their own sexual issues alone, just as their mothers did. Each year, married women in my practice tell me about turbulence in their marriage, or an affair, or an abortion and their decision to not go to their mothers—in the ways they normally do—for help with these issues. And they usually make almost the exact same comment as they explain their reasoning: "I could never tell her—she's never been through it." And I always ask, "How do you know?"

These things are not new to our generation. Just because a mother hasn't advertised these events doesn't mean she hasn't lived them out. Interestingly, as a counterpoint, when men in my practice report marital tension, rub-and-tug outings, or affairs, they never bring their fathers into it. I believe this has much to do with the fact that society makes room for male sexual experiences and transgressions. They understand they're a part of a community of men. Where men might feel guilt that they are betraying their wives, for example, women feel guilt *and* the extra weight of shame and isolation.

Marion, a stay-at-home mother with two children, had reached a point in her marriage where she felt "dead inside." Sex with her husband had become a chore, and over time she became less and less interested in being with him. Every time they tried to address the issue, they would have arguments that never resolved anything and left them each feeling hopeless. Like my client Alex, Marion too was very close to her mother, but she would not confide this state of affairs to her. She would say, "My parents have a great marriage. My mother has never felt anything like what I'm going through." She would say this even though she and her husband took great care never to fight in front of their children, and even though they put on the sunny couple face whenever they were out socially. About six months into her therapy, because she was so sad, Marion decided to fill her mother in on her unhappiness. She flew to Maine to spend a weekend with her, and over the course of their time together, her mother disclosed that Marion's father had had an affair when she was a little girl. She told her that for a long time she would recoil at his touch in the bedroom, but they hid their troubles when they were anywhere else. They made a commitment to stay together and work it out, and over the years they were able to grow into a marriage that made both of them very happy. Marion deeply appreciated her mother's candor, and was relieved when her mother offered to support her no matter how she decided to handle the disillusionment in her own marriage. She developed a new understanding of her mother, her father, and their love for each other, and she came away with a new respect for the complications of love relationships. It didn't fix her marriage, but it gave her a new perspective and made her feel less alone with it all.

Emily, a 30-year-old professor in a long-term relationship with her live-in partner, got pregnant. They were in love but had not been interested in having a family. However, with this surprise pregnancy their worlds were turned upside down, and they were undone at having to make such a heartbreaking decision. For weeks Emily hid her tears at work and cried herself to sleep as she went back and forth on whether to end the pregnancy or become a mother. She felt ashamed that she had allowed this to happen and didn't want to tell anyone, including her mother. Ultimately they saw abortion as the right choice for them; and Emily made the decision never to confide this to her mother, based on her belief that her mother would never have had an abortion.

There are women who have never told a soul they terminated a pregnancy—many of them mothers. In fact, 53 percent of the women who completed my abortion questionnaire were mothers.

The women I treat often express guilt and shame over difficult decisions they face in and around sexual relationships, such as contemplating ending a relationship with someone they love but with whom they no longer feel sexually compatible, or considering the termination of a pregnancy. They don't feel comfortable confiding these things to their mothers, and then because they learned to feel uncomfortable in that relationship, they often also choose not to confide in their girlfriends either. Just like us, what holds them back is a fear that they will be judged a bad person. They fear that how they are seen as women will be boiled down to an oversimplified derogatory characterization. She's fallen out of love with a perfectly lovely person? She's too picky—she thinks no one's good enough for her. She's getting an abortion? She's sexually careless, selfish, and perhaps morally bankrupt. Our daughters understand there is a good chance the men's roles in these scenarios will go largely unexamined and they, the women, will be seen as carrying the burden of these situations. Women in my practice who contemplate disclosing an unplanned pregnancy worry people will think, "It's her own fault— she let herself get pregnant." They are far less likely to anticipate that both partners will be held equally accountable, or to believe the man will be judged as careless for impregnating her. Women are concerned that the unique circumstances surrounding these deeply personal events won't be taken into consideration, and that the seriousness with which they make these decisions will be discounted. Their dread, just like their mothers', is that they won't be respected for having weighed and analyzed important, multi-layered situations and coming to a conclusion they feel, at that point in their lives, is right for them.

Daughters fear that the complexities of their sexual narratives won't be respected. However, in reading what daughters want to know about their mothers, we can see that they are *fully* aware of how complex *our* back stories may be. There is no obvious judgmental tone in their questions about their mothers' sexual lives. In fact it's often the opposite. Daughters demonstrate an appreciation for the complexity involved—an understanding that sexual choices are made in the context of complicated relationships, needs, priorities, and extenuating circumstances. Our daughters are showing us they have the emotional capacity to handle recognizing the intricacies we encounter as we live our lives. *Did she ever find the love she should have had with my father? Was she happy in her marriage? Satisfied and fulfilled—emotionally and sexually? How does she deal with the painful body memory of rape?* None of the daughters' questions in the list of what they most wanted to know about their mothers indicate searching for a place to lay blame or judgment. They reveal a nascent understanding ready to develop.

But remember the list of reasons our daughters don't ask us these questions. Not one of them said, "I don't ask because I couldn't handle it." Here are the three main reasons they don't ask: (1) They don't trust us to tell them the truth; (2) they don't want to hurt us; and (3) they don't want to be punished for asking. A study from Stanford University's Center for Research on Women found the same, citing that daughters' concern for their mothers' feelings kept them from asking them for help with contraception and sexual relationships. They feared "hurting or shocking their mothers, as well as the possibility of censure or reprisal."[1]

We do not intentionally put up this wall against our daughters. Yet an emotional block develops that often feels insurmountable. The consequence of our silence is that it causes our daughters to step into the role of protecting us, being careful of our vulnerabilities instead of receiving the intimacy they want by asking us about our lives.

Mothers aren't meant to be their daughters' best friends. I understand there are daughters who would be unnerved at learning something about their mothers' sexuality that they found to be upsetting. But I also know there are mothers who have not remained quiet but have actually devoted much thought to whether or not they should share something private with their daughters. My client Martine went through a trying period with her eldest daughter, Juliet, as they tried to weather a disclosure Martine made to her about her marriage. Throughout Juliet's teen years her mother and father had gone through an emotionally turbulent phase of their marriage, with the father moving out of the household several times. It took a toll on everyone in the family and created a lot of ill will between Juliet and her father. Her parents eventually reunited, but when Juliet was a freshman in college the marital discord resumed and Martine made two disclosures to her daughter. She told her that the martial tension was due to her father having had several affairs; and she told her that she was, and had always been, madly in love with him and would do everything in her power to hold the marriage together. Juliet was incredibly displeased with this because she couldn't bear to see her mother disregarded in this way. But Martine had had years to think about how she felt, what she wanted, and what she was willing to endure to have it. She was under no illusion that her marriage was solid in the traditional sense. What she did have, and what grounded her, was her conviction that she wanted to be with the man she loved, even under these circumstances. Even though Martine and Juliet continue to look at this situation from very different perspectives, because they talked about it, both mother and daughter have agreed to respect each other's feelings. This has allowed them to remain close and to feel heard and validated.

If we establish a truthful and open dialogue with our daughters from the time they are young girls, we'll give them the comfort level necessary to come to us to discuss issues of female sexuality if they choose to. And, because we'll already have seen the benefits of having given them information that has helped them, we'll have proven to ourselves that we can share, advise, and support them as we see fit. If we teach them the alphabet when they're young, it follows that as adults we'll be able to enjoy having increasingly complex conversations with them about what each of us reads. And if we teach them to respect sexuality when they're little, it can follow that as adults we can have increasingly complex conversations with them on sexuality and the role it plays in adulthood.

As I stated in the Introduction and with regard to the lists of questions for women to ask themselves in Chapter 1, mothers' and daughters' sexuality exists on the very same continuum. By that I mean that our sexuality and our sexual sense of self develops in sequence as our sexual experiences progress over our lives. Being born with female sexual organs is at one end of the continuum, and who we are sexually at the time of our death is at the other. In the middle, both mothers and daughters experience the confusion, heartbreak, and joy embedded in sexual relationships; we enjoy physical sensation that soothes and physical sensation that arouses; we share the need for sexual connection to express erotic love; and we measure the changes in our sexual selves over time. The only difference between our daughters and us is that, due to our being a generation apart in age, we are usually at different points of the continuum at any given time.

If we accept that mothers and daughters exist on the same sexual continuum, then we can accept that our daughters will likely encounter the same matters of sexuality that we have. Our daughters are growing up in a world very different from the one we were raised in. Technology has completely revamped the ways young people socialize, from being able to bare their souls on the internet to the ability to text nude photos. Sexual content of all sorts is at their fingertips. Clothing styles allow the showing of more and more skin at younger and younger ages. And our daughters can be pierced to the hilt and tatted up. But even taking into consideration mothers' and daughters' generational differences, the following are some of the realities not exclusive to mothers in the living out of a sexual life:

Daughters might question their sexuality. Daughters can get pregnant under conditions that are less than optimal. Daughters might be uncertain if they're with the right partner. Daughters do wonder how sex fits into all of the other complications of committed relationships, or, sometimes more importantly, in the absence of them. Daughters will likely come to see infidelity as the peanut butter to the jelly of supposed monogamy. Daughters do get molested. And about one in five daughters will be the victim of rape in her lifetime. Our awareness of these conditions can nullify the need to keep so many secrets.

What would happen if our daughters knew the information they privately want about our lives? Is it better for them to guess and draw their own conclusions about our sexual selves because that's somehow more palatable or survivable than being given the truth? Deciding what to disclose can't be determined with a simple formula. These decisions are personal, and can involve both risks and rewards. What if we disclose a secret that shatters a myth of us that they treasured? But, on the other hand, what if we could stop carrying the toxic shame of a secret—a secret our daughters wouldn't even see as malignant if it were revealed—and in fact may even be an emotional relief to them? When Marion found out her mother had also faced losing an erotic connection to her husband, she felt relieved and closer to her. And her mother, in comforting her daughter by sharing that she was not alone, also benefited. She was able to lift the weight of a secret off her shoulders and offer support to the daughter she loves dearly.

My intention isn't to pressure mothers into full disclosure at all costs. But what I do want to stress is that it's important that we make these decisions *thoughtfully and consciously*. I believe what's required of us at this time in history is to pause at these decision-making junctures to appreciate the importance of female sexuality and erotic life. We need to understand the tremendous value of sharing our knowledge with our daughters. We need to try to clear out as many of the historical and cultural cobwebs as we can from the way we communicate with our daughters and base our parenting decisions that relate to sexuality on a realistic and intimate understanding of our daughters and ourselves as unique, individual women.

If we erase our sexuality in our daughters' eyes we do us both a disservice. When we put our energy into the self-defeat of our own right to be sexually alive mothers, we defeat our daughters' chances of overcoming the discrimination that caused this closeting in the first place. As the adult daughters in my practice demonstrate, if we hide all of our sexual realities from our daughters because we fear it will destroy the illusion of our maternal purity or moral invulnerability, it may set our daughters on the same path of secrecy. Mothers who have had abortions and never talk about it out of shame might raise daughters who do the same. Mothers who whitewash the difficult sexual complexities of their marriages because they fear judgment might raise daughters who do too. Fear and shame will win again because our self-defeat is witnessed by them and often adopted as a life strategy for how to deal with their own sexuality and desire.

Our sexuality and desire deserve more reverence for their contribution to our very identities. Jessica Benjamin asserts that a mother who doesn't appreciate her own erotic life won't recognize it in her daughter.[2] And the profound relevance of desire is eloquently encapsulated by Deborah Tolman, who writes, "In desiring, I know that I exist."[3] If as mothers we understand the effect we have on our daughters, we would agree that there's no reason for us to encourage them to disengage from qualities of existence that are so valuable.

Using this awareness, we can see how our daughters would greatly benefit from the ways we can prepare them for appreciating desire's part in the texture of sexual relationships. We need to teach them that desire—in girls and women—is normal. This sounds simple, but because it isn't ever talked about, our daughters might see desire as something males can experience but is something dangerous for females. We should invite our daughters to join us in dialogues about matters of desire. If we create a safe space for them to explore these issues, they will feel less alone and confused by them. And when we share our own experience with desire and all its perplexities, we will offer them the sense of belonging to a community of females that they need. What does desire feel like in the body, and how do you reconcile that with what's going on in your head? What do you do when you desire someone who doesn't feel desire for you? What happens when you desire someone you "shouldn't"? What happens when you have desire, then it dies? How do you determine when to act on desire and when to try and quell it? These are just some of the talking points that might be of benefit to our daughters.

As we have these dialogues we need to keep in mind that the information we have for them should never be administered with a heavy hand but rather offered respectfully. Mothers don't always know what's best for their daughters—that is for daughters to determine; and no one wants a pushy mother who inserts herself into intimate matters. How we went through our own experiences might be incredibly different from how our daughters want to handle theirs, so we should see ourselves not as dictators of what they should do but as advisers who are always available. The maternal goal is to make clear a mutual understanding of our openness, not to impose our way of doing things. Assuming this position will make it easier for our daughters to recognize and respond to their own sexual sense of self. This will make everything they face easier, because it is always easier to be true to ourselves than to pretend otherwise.

Women in my study underscore the perplexities of love relationships and desire that point to why our daughters need our support. Quite a range of experience was found in response to what turned out to be one of my favorite parts of the study because of the way it outs the fantastic illogic of love. Here to represent the swings of passion long-term relationships can contain, are two women's thoughts. Each of them, the first in her forties, the second in her fifties, answers the following two-part question:

Q: In your most intense moments of love, what are your thoughts about your partner?

A: That he is the most wonderful man alive. And that I want to grow old with him.

Q: In your darkest moments of anything approaching hatred, what are your thoughts about your partner?

A: That he is the biggest ass alive. And that I want to grow old alone.

* * *

Q: In your most intense moments of love, what are your thoughts about your partner?

A: That he is the most wonderful, caring, kind, passionate man I could have dreamed of.

Q: In your darkest moments of anything approaching hatred, what are your thoughts about your partner?

A: That he is an absolute ignorant asshole with no social skills.

To the question "If you have fallen out of love, when did this occur?" a young woman wrote, *I don't think I've ever had intense moments of love....I've always had doubts. He's mean! He doesn't care! We aren't right for each other! This will never work!* A librarian in her late thirties said, *I wouldn't call it love, but he has demonstrated that he enjoys having me in his life and I feel bad that I don't reciprocate. I wish he'd fall over dead.* And one woman described the quality of the sex life in her 15-year marriage thusly: *It was fantastic until I didn't want him to touch me because I hated him.* Other ways desire can be unpredictable are confessed by the women in the affair questionnaire in response to the question "Were you surprised to find yourself in an affair or affairs?" One woman replied, *What good Catholic girl would dare?* A lawyer in her mid-sixties said, *At the beginning had you told me I would ever cheat on him, much less leave him, I would never have believed it. But we drifted apart to the point we were living parallel but separate lives.* Another woman stated, *It never felt like an affair to me. It just felt like falling in love.* And lastly, a 48-year-old professor wrote, *I had thought of myself as rational, disciplined, and monogamous. Falling in love brought on a kind of madness—I could observe myself doing things that I knew were wrong and foolish and at the same time I had never been happier.*

Hopefully our daughters will know long-lasting and fulfilling love. But the complexities described by these women are looming out there for our daughters. The discomfiting mysteries of passion and the way it appears and disappears in our relationships can cause great upheaval in our lives. In times of such upheaval our support systems take on added importance. If our daughters don't feel comfortable turning to us, and this has influenced them to be reluctant to turn to their girlfriends, their upheaval becomes even more pronounced. Cut off from an ability to confide the realities of their lives, they will be on their own to manage under the strain of the upheaval itself as well as having fewer resources for comfort. When we hear the realities of what can happen for women in our relationships—truths we aren't always inclined to share with each other—it's no wonder our daughters secretly want our help.

If we combine all we're up against in facing more frank sexual dialogues—sexist cultural restrictions, fear of judgment, and no road map for how to go about it—is it any wonder mothers and daughters are cautious walking this ground? It should come as no surprise that the adult daughters in my study, even the youngest of them, who were raised by mothers of the "postfeminist" era, leave sexual questions as the ones unasked.

What's noteworthy about these unasked questions is that they beg two others: *What* are we teaching our daughters about being female? And what are we *withholding* from them that might be useful for them to know in the face of all these challenges?

Are we teaching them that they should feel uneasy or ashamed of female sexuality? Daughters know that the things we mothers feel happy with and proud of tend to be easily shared with them. Things that are tinged with shame, regret, fear, or a sense of violating social decorum are typically harder to share. So what should a daughter infer if we are silent on sexuality? Should she assume that her curiosity about her mother's sexuality is something unnatural? Should a daughter contemplating the loss of her own virginity not wonder about that of the woman who gave birth to her? Should a daughter questioning her sexuality have to go through that alone without her mother, who is also a sexual being? Are we subtly encouraging our daughters to drive their own sexuality underground right along with ours? And to what extent are we complicit in teaching them to expect that their sexuality will vanish from the public eye as soon as they're married, become mothers, or begin to age?

Even though the thought that our daughters could face them is hard to contemplate, abortion and sexual trauma also deserve our attention. Even if we had an abortion and feel we made the right decision for ourselves, it's still common to feel sadness or guilt. Therefore, some of us may choose to keep it private. But what of our daughters? If they found themselves in a position to consider abortion, would they wish to have us as an adviser or support? And would we want to know in order to be there for them? If we've kept an abortion secret, how would that impact our daughters' decision to confide in us or not? Such impasses are difficult in and of themselves, but they become even more difficult if they are shrouded in secrecy.

The concern that our daughters could one day have to confront rape is also a very uncomfortable thought for mothers to contemplate. Yet the 2004 National Crime Victimization Survey posted on the Rape, Abuse and Incest National Network (RAINN) website reports, "About 44% of rape victims are under age 18, and 80% are under age 30."[4] These percentage clusters soundly cover our daughters' age ranges and once again force the question, Have we set the ground for them to trust us enough to come to us for help? We first approached this topic in Chapter 4 from the angle of masturbation and establishing a baseline of sexual health, and here it arises again. From a mother's perspective, if we were raped, maybe we wouldn't want to discuss it with our daughters. But could that prevent us from seeing the possibility that, as with the women in my study, our daughters might want to learn more about how we cope with it? And if we knew that, would it influence us to consider speaking about it? Or what if we wish we could talk to our daughters about our rape, but hold back for fear of the very same thing our daughters might fear—not wanting to upset anyone?

It's a personal call whether or not to talk about such loaded topics. But the fact remains that these events will confront women again and again. They'll affect women and girls we'll never meet, and they'll affect the women and girls we love. Understanding their prevalence and coupling that with our daughters' desire to learn from us can help us move away from the shame and isolation that used to motivate our silence, and allow us to break into a space of sexual respect and dignity. Whatever our decisions, as long as they're made thoughtfully, taking into consideration the needs of both mother and daughter, we should respect them.

WHY OUR DAUGHTERS WANT TO KNOW OUR SEXUAL NARRATIVES

Giving our daughters too much sexual detail about our lives, even as adults, can be overwhelming and consequently is usually not a good idea. But that isn't what our daughters are asking for. They're not asking us about coital positions or how we want our partners to perform oral sex on us. They want to know who we are as sexual *beings*—they want to know the *erotic truth* about us. They want to know who we are as women in love, women at crossroads, women in trouble, and women who've been victimized. They want to hear about things like which sexual choices we regret, which we merely abide, and which we wouldn't change for the world. They want to know if we've ever been fulfilled in our love lives, and if it's possible for couples to stay connected over time. They want to know if trauma is survivable. They want to know if our allegiance to our own happiness is supported, tempered, or undermined by our allegiance to our partners. They want to better understand us *in our entirety*, and to go to school on us, feeling a sense of female community around these huge, sweeping issues. What is bad about their wanting to know any of these things as they try to navigate their own lives? And what is bad about a mother feeling close enough to her daughter to be able to talk about any of this content of life?

Our daughters know we have life experience and knowledge for them around sexuality and all its beguiling complications. And they also know we're not easily giving it up. Even for them.

Chapter Six

Saving Our Daughters from Our Best Intentions

We often focus on body image from the perspective of its link to eating disorders in adolescent girls, and we hope these are short-term difficulties they "grow out of." We think that, once they abstain from dieting, yo-yoing, bingeing, or starving, their weight will stabilize and their lives will be normal. But the drag of a negative body image on a female's sense of self isn't always confined to one short period in her life.

Developmentally speaking, adolescence is often merely the time these disorders come into full bloom because they've been cultivated in our girls all the years leading up to that point. (This does not include eating disorders that are symptomatic of sexual, physical, and emotional abuse or rape.) The reason these disorders erupt in adolescence is because maturation calls it forth—girls' awareness of their social and sexual presence becomes more acute just as the changes in their bodies become more striking. According to the *Wall Street Journal*, recent studies have shown disturbing spikes in prepubescent girls' fixation with thinness, with one study reporting that 81 percent of ten-year-old girls had already dieted to lose weight, and another finding that girls as young as five have a preoccupation with body image. It also reports anorexia is on the rise, and the incidence of bulimia is three times higher than it was 30 years ago.[1] In addition to starting earlier than we tend to think, these problems also stay with us longer than we'd like to admit. Eating disorder clinics are currently treating significantly more women over 30, with one clinic recording a 400 percent increase in admissions of women over 40 in a recent ten-year span.[2] From five-year-old girls to women in their sixties, these statistics represent millions of females. By simple extended logic, they reveal the struggles of millions of *mothers and daughters*.

As unsettling as these statistics are, they depict only part of the problem. It's also important to remember that the way a girl or woman lives with a negative body image affects her life well beyond the clinical parameters of anorexia and bulimia. Some women continue to live with eating disorders well into their adult life, many of them successfully hiding it from their family and friends for decades. But the impairments in living aren't experienced only by those with active disorders. I often treat adult women who had eating disturbances in their high school or college years, and although the behavior may have stopped, their emotional connection to their bodies remains entangled in shame and a battle for control over self-worth. Girls and women can also struggle with body image without ever having met the diagnostic criteria for these disorders, and still find themselves plagued by a daily focus on what they hate about themselves. As we witnessed with sexuality, body image will affect a daughter's self-worth and her ability to be comfortable in her body in all areas of her life, because if she has a negative body image, then throughout everything she engages in she will, quite literally, be in a body that torments her. While culture is accountable for foisting arbitrary and unreasonable expectations on our daughters, our role as mothers also needs to be examined for the contributions we make to our daughters' vulnerability to succumb to them.

As a psychoanalyst, I hear lots of amazing and upsetting stories of all kinds. Stories of anxiety, depression, and grief, love stories with happy endings, breakthroughs, and triumphs of spirit. But over the last 25 years, there's only one type of problem I can honestly say I believe I've heard reported in some form every single day I've practiced. My female clients reveal it explicitly and implicitly, and my male clients regularly refer to it when talking about the women they love: women who have internalized negative body images, with ensuing feelings of self-doubt and low self-worth. Although patriarchy remains the wellspring of sexism, what's come to my attention through the women's stories I've listened to is that we now learn much of this self-loathing from the women around us—most destructively, our mothers. To help combat this, all women, not only mothers, need to be mindful that girls learn to be women in three ways: (1) *through what we say to them*, (2) *through what they observe in us*, and (3) *through what they observe in our interactions with each other.*

Much has already been written on the physical and emotional harm associated with poor body image in teens. But little attention is paid to the distance our fixation with body image creates in the mother-daughter relationship—a distance that in turn disrupts our daughters' relationship to themselves and others throughout their lives. Daughters disclose the power we as mothers have over how they see their bodies. We convey it through our competition with them, the expression of our own self-loathing in front of them, and our pressuring of them to "improve" their bodies. We need to be aware that along with the long-term toll this takes on our daughters' sense of self, it also undermines our mother-daughter relationships because our daughters fear we don't really love them for who they are. And if they believe they are a disappointment to us, their prospects for feeling worthy of the love of others is significantly diminished. Their fear of being seen as a disappointment will bleed into their other relationships, most specifically their sexual ones. Depending on the intensity and pervasiveness of the body pressures we place on them, or on ourselves in front of them, our daughters can come to have an underlying belief that they are unworthy, undesirable, and unlovable unless they look a certain way. They also witness how we don't value ourselves as we are, which makes us less idealizable as women, and sets them up to lose respect for us. Our daughters keep these fears and beliefs to themselves because they are devastating and humiliating; therefore, they're unlikely to share them with us. They also have little faith that we will be able to support them. It's hard for our daughters to imagine we can help them inspire confidence in themselves when they see we can't do it for ourselves.

The divide this tension creates between mothers and daughters isn't just caused by blatant body critiques that are easy for us to spot, such as the statement "You'd be so much prettier if you lost weight." Other forms of communication are also the culprits. A mother who works out excessively because she says she wants to be "fit" can be seen by her daughter as obsessed by thinness. It doesn't even have to be talked about. It only needs to be noticed. Obsessions like these create distance rather than closeness because they consume all of our energy and distract us from engaging meaningfully in our relationships and other parts of our lives. Sometimes in an attempt to be like her mother, a daughter will feel she has to do what her mother does. A shared workout obsession like this can seem like a bond, but it isn't one based on health. It is based on pursuing the *appearance* of health, one that camouflages the true driving force of both mother and daughter: self-loathing. True closeness can't exist in a relationship based on self-loathing because it's a destructive force that alienates us from ourselves, and we can't have a true connection with another person if we aren't even connected to ourselves.

Distance can also be fostered in more subtle ways, for example when we think we're complimenting our daughters. One of my clients, a journalist in her early 30s, illustrates how this works. "Whenever I see my mother she always has to comment on how thin and beautiful my body is. Then she makes some reference to how she used to have a body like mine but now it's gone to shit. It always makes me really uneasy, and this is hard for me to say, but it grosses me out. I want her to pull it together so I don't pity her. It seems like she's saying something nice about me, but it isn't about her being happy for me at all. It's about her feeling less than. You know what else? *I* think we still have the same body. We look alike. So when she says those things it brings me down and I get self-conscious. I'll spend weeks after I visit her analyzing my body, and then I hate myself for being like her."

In instances such as this, our daughters read our conscious or unconscious competitive feelings toward them. They also notice the lack of acceptance we feel over our own bodies. As this client makes clear, daughters have strong emotional reactions to this dynamic. It puts them in an unwinnable situation. Their connection to us is jeopardized because they stand to lose something no matter how they handle it. If they embrace their bodies with a healthy attitude, either they fear we'll become more jealous and distance ourselves, or they'll feel guilty because they're leaving us behind in the pursuit of their own health. On the other hand, if they do things to sabotage their bodies—hide them, abuse them, pursue extreme weight-control activities—in an attempt to make us feel less badly about ourselves, they surrender their body integrity to us and lose themselves. They will either end up pitying or resenting our inability to be more confident, or they will join us in that lack of confidence.

The responses to my body image questionnaire show that women feel these problems across different generations. Most women reported spending 30 to 40 percent of every day thinking about body image, and 46 percent of them said they focused on it because their mothers did. The women who completed this questionnaire ranged in age from 18 to 47 and were gay, straight, and bisexual, with African America, Asian American, and Caucasian women being represented. (No Hispanic women completed this questionnaire, and I hope that is a sign of their positive body image.) Taken together they represent how widespread and long-standing our focus on how we look is. It isn't something only "insecure" women feel; it's very much in the mainstream. In each generation women reported the same problem. A woman in her twenties wrote, *I grew up in a home where being thin was over-stressed by my mother. She was always talking about weight or losing weight.* A woman in her thirties stated, *My mother focused/es on it incessantly.* And another in her forties said, *I was groomed from an early age by my mother, aunts, and grandmother to look a certain way (weight, clothing, hairstyle, makeup, jewelry, etc.).* Women shared what it felt or feels like to live under this influence from their mothers: *I think my mother gave me a complex, and I resent it....[She] put too much emphasis on weight. To this day, I don't feel adequate as a result of being overweight. I also feel she favors my sister, who is not overweight. I resent this. I also resent how small my mother has made me feel over the years....I wish she would just accept me as I am.* And one woman conveyed how it feels to try not to repeat her mother's mistakes in her own mothering, confiding, *It's quite difficult some days. It seems that the thinner I am, the more obsessed I am about my looks. It is a constant struggle not to pass this anxiety on to my eight-year-old daughter.* As we can see from my client's narrative and the feedback from women in the study, our deconstruction of our daughters affects them regardless of their size and body type.

As women, we can't help but be affected by the sexist attitudes we grew up with, but we chase physical perfection with a fervor that belies some of the strides we've made toward equality. The issue at hand at this point in history is whether we are willing to evaluate our own behavior in an effort to lessen the harmful impact of that sexism, especially on behalf of our daughters.

Today, conversations about the body are one of the primary ways women communicate with each other, and it's important to step back and realize that it's harmful when it's somehow degrading. It can be part of what we talk about, but it doesn't have to be so central and negative. The way we express the deconstruction of our bodies is pervasive. It crops up everywhere. I remember one night when my daughter was 11 and I came home to find our Rubenesque cat, Purr, sitting on the hall table gazing at herself in the mirror. My daughter had noticed her before I did, and told me Purr had been checking herself out for quite some time. When I smiled and asked my daughter what on earth she thought the cat was thinking, she said, "Does this fur make my butt look big?" And after I took a second to process this, I asked her where she'd heard someone say something like that. "The Disney Channel," she replied.

We express how we feel about our bodies as women in all sorts ways. Think about the meaning of a casual phrase like "I hate my thighs." It may sound lightly self-deprecating, but it also says the speaker hates a part of her body to which she's inextricably attached. We assess each other's physicality and judge women who are overweight. We try to trick our bodies into "looking" healthy by developing bad habits that result in eating disorders.

We are complicit in our own objectification. What leads to this culture of competition and lack of generosity with ourselves? A woman in my study pronounces,

> *It's hard for women, because I think so much of our self-worth is based on appearance. But is this coming from society? Or is it really coming from ourselves? If we could all love ourselves and each other and appreciate all the beauty (in and out) I think we would be better off. I don't think this stuff matters to men as much as women think it does—male attention is not what is most important to women. Generally most of the paranoia about looks is caused by women competing with and comparing themselves to other women and the perception of a hierarchy of looks.*

Through our language and behavior we confirm self-loathing and the deconstruction of ourselves, and we teach it to each other and our daughters without realizing it. In the Introduction I called out how this occurs through seemingly innocent statements like, "I was bad today. I had cake." What follows are more overt examples of how it gets enacted.

One of my clients, Rachel, an actress in her early twenties, has flown to Los Angeles to stay with her parents while she attends the premiere of a movie she's in. Lights are twinkling and the magic of the event is all around her. She's dressed to the nines, but thinking to herself, "I hate the way I look. I should have worn the other outfit... no... stop it Rachel... focus on this amazing night. Turn off the tape in your head and live in the moment." The film has been critically acclaimed in *The New York Times*, and she's trying to remind herself that she is incredibly excited and proud. When the movie is over her mother comes up to her and says, "Great movie, honey!" Then she leans in, lowers her voice to a whisper and continues, "It's a shame, though, that the outfits they put you in were so unflattering and made you look heavy.... " shaking her head to convey how upsetting this misfortune is. In that moment, who Rachel is in the world evaporates. Her mother doesn't see her. There is no daughter, no actress, no affirmation of all that's great in her, no shared celebration, no maternal pride. There is only an outline of the mother's perception of a size and a shape—a crime-scene chalk line encircling the space where a living body used to be. In those few words we see a mother who can't access the fullness of who her daughter is, and consequently, a daughter who's denied access to the fullness of her mother, because the filter through which her mother values her is so fine as to exclude all else. The final consequence is a daughter who can't be free to celebrate herself.

It's amazing how one comment can be so destructive. I know from women in my practice that each time a comment like this is made, a girl or woman will remember it vividly forever. And if such comments are made repeatedly, they will be archived in a volume set in her mind. When this happens, not only does it make one unable to celebrate oneself, but another one of the greatest things about celebrating something dies: there is no joy in sharing it with others. A preoccupation with shame takes hold in the space that should be full of mutual commemoration. If a mother's outlook penetrates her daughter's sense of self in these ways, how many special occasions are vulnerable to having their potential for joy sideswiped by body image? Life is full of them: dances, dates, recitals and weddings, speeches, presentations, the first day at a new job, pregnancy...the list goes on. These are the times our daughters should be bursting with pride, confidence, or happiness, and looking to us to see their joy mirrored in our eyes. They should not have to instead be transfixed by how they wish they were different and less alone in their shame.

Another client, Madeline, a jewelry designer in her thirties, says that even though she loves her family, it's hard to visit her home because she knows her mother will focus on her weight. Her feeling is common among the women in my practice. Weeks before family holidays, she starts to obsess about it, and the secret bulimia with which she's lived for more than half of her life kicks in. "It's revving up again, as usual. My mom is calling about Thanksgiving plans and I'm already a wreck wondering how I'm going to lose weight before I have to see her. I only threw up once the entire summer and now I've binged twice since our session last week." Soon, as is the case with many of my clients, she's so vulnerable she needs backup to help her cope with the shame and depression she feels, and out come the martinis and Marlboro Lights. She knows they're bad for her health and they only make things worse, but she hopes they provide her momentary distraction from food and her thoughts. Her mind is constantly cycling through questions she has to answer in order to be prepared. How much weight can she lose before Thanksgiving? What outfits can she take to make herself look the thinnest? When her mother makes comments, what, if anything, will she say in response? Her preoccupation with her body is as insistent as it is understandable, because it has become tied in with the attendant fantasy any of us would have: I would be more loved by my mother if I were thinner. Madeline sees her mother as beautiful and slender, and Madeline will never look like her, she thinks. She wants to be close to her mother, but she's tormented by feeling reduced to a number on a scale, first by her mother, and now by herself.

Madeline illuminates the side of body image women live with that we don't usually contemplate. Her relationship to her mother around this area of self-worth and self-esteem doesn't only affect her sense of herself in her body. We can see that much of the autumn is consumed by it because she has to plan and work on how to protect herself from her mother's scrutiny. It takes a toll on her life in general. The weeks leading up to Thanksgiving she feels increasingly raw so she doesn't want to be with her friends as much. She realizes how preoccupied she is and she knows this makes it harder for her to really connect with them. Then they'll want to know what's wrong, and she won't want to tell them, so it's simply easier for her to avoid them. Madeline is also distracted at work. It's harder for her to get in touch with her creativity, and she'd rather shop online for a new outfit she'd maybe feel safe and good in than keep up with her paperwork. She also has to contend with her guilt over too much smoking and drinking, which interrupts her management of her health. The whole idea of celebrating a holiday with family and friends has gone up in smoke. She adores her brothers and sisters, but the topical tension with her mother dims her ability to let herself go enough to enjoy them. So, sadly, her siblings' ability to enjoy her is also dimmed. Lastly, when she goes home, all of the emotional life she has devoted to bracing herself for the visit will be unapparent to everyone around her because she will act as if everything is fine.

Recently, I met a friend for lunch. I had already been seated when she called me to let me know she was running late. I had fifteen minutes to kill so I took out a book and began to read, but my reading was interrupted when two women who looked to be in their 40s were seated at the table next to me. The entire time I waited for my friend, they talked of *nothing* but dieting. Current diets, past diets, diets they would never try, diets they might consider in the future, diets that come with their own food programs, diets you shop for for yourself...Long after my friend arrived they remained engrossed in this all-important topic.

We often conceive of body image as a solitary preoccupation for a woman—the subject of an internal conversation she runs in her own head. But audible dialogues between women are all around us like white noise we barely notice. When we do tune into them, we tend to see them as nothing more than casual conversations between adult women. But women are having these conversations in the vicinity of children, who pick them up on their own radio frequencies. We're having them in restaurants when we're sitting at a table for two that happens to be next to a table of teenage girls. We're talking about it on playgrounds while our kids play or on the telephone while they're studying nearby. It doesn't occur to us that while we're engaging in these deconstructions of ourselves we're actually broadcasting them to other ears, and helping shape attitudes on self-worth.

On another occasion, I was having breakfast by myself in a quiet hotel restaurant. There was only one other person there, a middle-aged woman who told the waiter she was waiting for someone just as another middle-aged woman entered to join her. It became clear that it was a business breakfast and, although they'd had a phone relationship, that this was the first time they'd met in person. As they greeted each other, one of the women referred to being in town for her daughter's college graduation. The other woman exclaimed, "You don't look old enough to have a daughter that age!" to which she responded that she had an even older daughter who just had a baby, so she was also a new grandmother. Again, the woman commented in an exaggerated tone, "You're *kidding!* You don't look old enough to be a grandmother!" Age takes center stage and everything else disappears. There is no acknowledgment of the birth, becoming a new grandmother, or the graduation. What should be some of the most joyful moments in life are no match for the jubilation inspired by female youth.

Aging offers certain rewards that youth cannot. It represents the culmination of our efforts in building self-knowledge, families, friendships, careers, and the sense of self that comes from facing whatever adversity we may have encountered. Aging is to be honored. Youth certainly has its own set of rewards, but to dwell on them to the exclusion of those that come later in life causes a stagnation of the self. It keeps us from experiencing an appreciation of living an *entire* life, not just the beginning. When we're really old we will likely measure our lives by how well we loved, how well we were loved, and by what we created, whether that be family, work, art, or friendships. Even if we have chosen to have them, we will probably not measure our lives collagen injection by collagen injection.

Several things might be helpful to keep in mind as we confront the challenge of trying not to undermine ourselves and our daughters in these ways. The first is not to feel guilty. Each of us does this undermining, consciously or unconsciously, because we've learned to; it's the cultural color in which we've all been dyed. It's impossible not to be tinted by the negative, unrealistic ways women and girls are viewed because it's so pervasive it's molecular. And while it may be frustrating that we all do it, at least there's a comfort in it too, because it means we can all fumble through trying to improve the situation together without feeling shame. Also, in my clinical experience, undermining, at its deepest level, is usually motivated not by a wish to hurt someone but by a desire to make ourselves feel emotionally safe. It begins with our best intentions. *We feel safe when we have the illusion of being beyond scrutiny, and needing to feel safe is the cornerstone of all human behavior.* The undermining itself isn't helpful, but the psychological goal it's hoping to achieve is necessary in maintaining mental health. So the task at hand for mothers is to help our daughters reach the goal of safety through means other than this undermining.

Understanding the psychological mechanics of scrutiny can help us move past our fixation with body image and whatever cultural forces happen to be dictating the definition of beauty for any particular generation. One doesn't have to believe she is the most perfect creature to have walked the face of the earth. What's needed is a realistic appreciation of who we are. That is where a true sense of safety can come from.

Here is how one 24-year-old woman describes searching for that appreciation on her own terms, in the physical appearance questionnaire:

I can be very self-conscious about my looks and my body, but certainly not as much as I used to be when I was a teenager. As a black female, I have an alternate standard of beauty to live up to. Most black women are appreciated for their 5'5" frame, curvy hips, and ample bottom, à la Beyoncé. I, on the other hand, am 5'8" (yet look much taller), skinny and flat as a pancake on my backside. I always joke that somewhere in rural Kentucky there is a white girl walking around with my ass. Note to Becky Sue: I want my butt back! I have come a long way from the hatred that I used to have for my body growing up. I despised my figure and figured the best way to hide from it was to wear baggy clothes, which I did throughout most of my teenage years. Most girls who do not have the body are able to make up for it in other ways, but not me. I was not particularly pretty. I am not light skinned and I do not have the light eyes and "good" hair that years of self-hatred have led many black people (especially young boys) to adopt as the ideal form of beauty. During my teen years and even through my first year of college, I abused my skin with whitening products in the hopes of becoming beautiful to someone else other than God. It was not until my sophomore year of college, when I was introduced to a number of women's studies and African American studies courses, that I started appreciating my physical self. The funny thing is I was so busy trying to change my looks to please others that I failed to realize that I thought I was beautiful. I loved my dark skin and even wished for it to be darker. In it, I saw the skin of ancient African royalty and the admiration that they were given without asking. There are days when I still compare myself to other women who fit the mold of America's beauty, but when I realize I am heading on that detrimental road, I force myself to look in the mirror and take a realistic look at the real me. When I do, I start to value my never-ending dimples, my nine-hundred-watt smile, my defined cheekbones, and my expressive eyes.

This woman models for us how, if we work on it, temporal cultural restrictions on identity can recede to allow more room for our personal discovery of what our own distinctive beauty means to us. She also illustrates how the introduction of alternate perceptions, like those she gained in her women's and African American studies, can afford us a healthier take on ourselves. This will benefit us exponentially, because when we have a healthier take on ourselves, that health extends into our participation in healthier relationships, and a healthier ability to partake in all other endeavors of our work and social life.

Another woman, a 40-year-old mother in graduate school, gives us a different example of experiencing comfort and self-worth in her own way.

The only time I start judging my body is when I'm around my mother. I feel her looking at me and comparing me to my sister. I've reached a point in my life where I'm more in awe of what my body can do, rather than [worried about] how it looks. I believe yoga brought me to this place. As a result, my body might look better. Although, I don't know if it really does or if my judgment is coming from a much more loving place. It comes with age. In a way I could say I've "given up," but it feels more like I've released myself of all the pressure. In life's long list of stresses, it's nice to be free of this one.

This woman's shift in perception helps move her from judgment all the way to awe. It's a testimony to the power of the mind and what is possible if we are determined. Maybe miracles won't occur, but improvements in how we feel in our lives definitely can. Both of these women can inspire us to pursue healthy realism as we practice pulling back on the ways we scrutinize.

Scrutiny is what lives at the root of our insecurities about our physical self, and here is how it works psychodynamically: When we scrutinize ourselves, we already know how we'd like to be different. At its healthiest, this dissatisfaction might motivate us to make a change in our lives that would work toward that goal. In other words, sometimes we use scrutiny to irritate ourselves into action that may enhance our confidence. A simple example of this would be allowing our irritation with a current haircut to motivate us to get a different one we feel better in. It then would follow that we would feel a higher level of comfort, which in turn would bring about a greater sense of safety. But scrutiny can be destructive when we constantly examine our perceived flaws. Then, scrutiny undermines our sense of self by breeding self-loathing, because our fixation prohibits its transformation into the more comfortable state of feeling safe. A psychological fixation is like a car that's stuck in the mud. The wheels spin and spin and spin but the car never goes anywhere. With fixation, we think and think and think, but because we're trapped in the same thought pattern, no change can click in to help us move forward. Instead we stay stuck, spinning our wheels on the power with which we imbue each flaw. This is what's most dangerous for our daughters and us, as the stories of Rachel and Madeline prove. When it comes to scrutinizing other women or our daughters, our scrutiny comes with either a desire to feel superior (keeping ourselves safe), or a desire to preemptively protect them from what we imagine will be the even harsher scrutiny of others (keeping them safe). If we, or our daughters, are the prettiest or thinnest, we feel safer because we believe it makes us more desirable, acceptable, and lovable. And why wouldn't we? It's what our culture has raised us to believe.

Understanding women's misdirected attempts to feel safe can encourage us to have more empathy and patience with each other as we try to develop healthier ways to perceive ourselves. If we can allay our ingrained self-loathing and redirect our efforts toward healthier ways of feeling emotionally safe, the problem of overscrutiny will begin to fade. The reality, of course, is that there's nothing any of us can do to guarantee emotional safety. But trying to live our lives feeling comfortable and balanced in who we are is the best shot we, and our daughters, have at being both safe and happy. There are fundamental changes we can make in order to feel a more genuine sense of that comfort and safety, which will reduce our *need* to sabotage our daughters and ourselves.

Inauthentic pride, which masks our insecurities, is competitive and withholding—it's what creates rivalry between women; but when we feel authentic pride in who we are, the need for sabotage becomes obsolete, because authentic pride is generous. The more generous we are with ourselves and others, the healthier we become. We often fear making changes toward health, though, because we worry we'll be somehow restricted, as with dieting, for example. But restriction is the problem here, not the solution. We need to expand the ways in which we feel genuine pride and comfort in all directions beyond "beauty." Millions of women work hard to try to feel beautiful, and some feel they never attain it. Other women feel they have youthful beauty and try to hold on to it for dear life. If we believe that all we can be valued for is beauty, and then for whatever reason it isn't there, there is nothing left for us to value. If we restrict our self-worth to that and only that, we automatically place ourselves in an all-or-nothing situation where we will always be at risk of losing the one thing we think we have going for us.

I'm not saying that moving away from these sexist attitudes is easy. They've been entrenched for generations. But it's invigorating to know that the changes required of us at this point in history will not constrict our freedoms. They will open us up to having more. We need to feel a healthy sense of entitlement to everything outside the illusion of physical perfection and appreciate the distinction our imperfections give us. We need to embrace food as a source of nourishment and pleasure, not weight. We need to feel entitled to speak our minds, follow our hearts, and celebrate our strengths. We need to move away from the ways we martyr ourselves by constantly giving out, and instead give care, time, and comfort to ourselves, understanding that to do so isn't selfish but self-sustaining. In this spirit we need to grow comfortable being given to by others so we feel balance in our relationships. We need to accept receiving pleasure on all fronts—especially sexually. Women don't deserve to experience erotic vitality because we are young or beautiful. We deserve to experience it because it is an elemental part of being human.

The fulfillment of these needs should come first and foremost in the way we see ourselves, and in the way we raise our daughters. In our maternal role we need to bolster our daughters' ability to find balance between an appropriate amount of vanity and society's pressurized standards of body image and beauty. It's all right to have some vanity. Wanting to feel and look good is part of being self-confident. And to not feel on some level compelled to physically conform to some slice of the society we live in would be unwise, because if we didn't we'd feel ostracized and miserable. The trouble is our myopic focus. When we view ourselves through that lens, we teach our daughters to do the same. The ways we collude in keeping our physicality in the foreground while everything else about us is blurred, creates an imbalance we need to rectify. The true beauty of womanhood lies in each of us deciding for herself what that balance is.

Taking all of this into consideration, how can a mother go about helping dilute the pressures of body image for her daughter? As suggested, don't dissect and judge your own body parts or those of other women in front of her, and don't do it to hers. When she asks for your opinion on how she looks, teach her to be true to herself: Ask *her* how *she* feels her best, then ask what it is about that that makes her feel good. This way you'll learn what's important to her, and open up a dialogue around these issues.

When you give your daughter a compliment, be careful to avoid language that reinforces the stereotype that thin equals best. Better to say "you look great" or "that really flatters you," rather than "that makes you look so skinny!" The goal is for her to feel confident and happy, not thin.

Focus on her feelings and thoughts so that she experiences herself as three-dimensional. If your interest falls on body image and beauty, hers will too. Instead, teach her to respect her own take on things; let *your interest in her perspective* nudge physical appearance off the altar of worship. Teach her to respect her own take on things. Devote your attention to qualities you value that have nothing to do with her physicality, like her intelligence, empathy, humor, intuition, forthrightness, kindness, musical or artistic ability, or athleticism. And when you talk with her ask questions and make statements that draw these qualities out:

> What do you think?
> What do you feel?
> How do you want to handle it?
> What feels right to you?
> That's a great point.
> I disagree, but I see your point.
> Tell me more.
> And finally, one statement to make whenever it can be done in earnest:
> I admire that in you.

The more confident a girl is, the better able she'll be to hold her own against social pressures. If a girl is supported in being whole, maybe she'll grow into a woman who appreciates the *singularity* of her body and the complexities of her mind and her heart.

SEXUALITY AND BODY IMAGE

Understanding that it's an uphill climb, how do we reconcile for our daughters and ourselves our struggles with "beauty" and body image when it comes to their impact on our sexual expression? Are our daughters pretty and thin enough to be arousing and aroused? Are we? Is that what it takes to be worthy of giving and accepting erotic love?

If we invest too much of our identity in the belief that we are only worthy under a specific set of physical criteria, then we dismiss the premise that both beauty and sexual attraction are highly subjective.

What attracts us, as well as what attracts others to us, is particular to each individual, and to not embrace this reality profoundly shortchanges the mysteries of how desire works. Men in my practice often describe being drawn to and aroused by the very things their lovers find to be "ugly." What to one person is fat, to another person is soft. Where one is drawn to dark features, another is drawn to fair. There is the collective, culturally manufactured definition of "beauty," and then there is true beauty, which can be none other than subjective and different for everyone. Stopping to remind ourselves that individual perceptions of beauty exist will make our pressures lighter. We could be far more open to acknowledging our subjective experience of what is beautiful in us, as well as to acknowledging others' subjective experience of what they find to be beautiful in us.

Here is a narrative to champion that philosophy. One woman in my study who responded to many of the questionnaires laced each of them with comments about how painful it was for her that she was judged for being clinically overweight. She felt belittled by the glares of others. But she was also married to a man who couldn't get enough of her, and with whom she felt beautiful and womanly. In one of her responses she wrote: *Sometimes, like when I'm standing in line at the bank and someone is looking at me like I'm disgusting, I want to turn to them and let them know that about an hour earlier I was having my third screaming orgasm with the man who tells me how much he loves me every day.* By embracing the different ways our bodies are beautiful, we will be able to participate more fully in our lives, and our sexual relationships will become more intimate. Unfortunately, I usually hear the opposite from the men in my practice, who express their frustration with the distance created by their wives' or girlfriends' negative deconstruction of themselves. Many report feeling beaten down by women's need to criticize their bodies. Here are three examples from my caseload that reveal men's common experience of women who have internalized objectification.

"I love my wife's breasts. They're beautiful to me but she doesn't like them. When she's naked, she's always covering them up, folding her arms in front of them, even though I constantly tell her they're incredible. Her self-consciousness really gets to me. It makes her shy in bed. I love her, but you know what? I'm getting a little tired of it. She constantly dismisses me when I compliment her and I'm starting to wonder why I even bother to reassure her when she makes it so clear that it doesn't matter to her what I say, or how I see her."

"My girlfriend is hung up on her cellulite. When we're getting ready to make love I can tell it's all she's thinking about. I think she looks great. I never even noticed the cellulite before she started pointing it out to me. The bummer is, that since she's constantly complaining about it, now I do see it. It still doesn't bother me like it bothers her, but what does bug me is the fact that it's become this huge focal point in our sex life."

"My wife is pretty subdued, maybe even prudish in bed. She thinks she's fat. We always have to have the lights off. It's aggravating. I feel like she won't let me in."

Women in my study support these experiences with confessions about their sense of their bodies: *I feel insignificant and unworthy of the love my boyfriend shows me. And I wish that I could feel content in my own skin. Having a loving, supportive partner who thinks I'm perfect does not seem to make it easier, so I'm not sure what will.*

We women need to shift our focus away from the dread of how others will perceive us, to come back to our own centers. What turns *us* on? When does *our* desire ignite? Where do *our* longings fall? We would be far happier if we did this, because our dread isn't protecting us. It's putting our relationships in jeopardy in addition to causing our self-worth to plummet even further. We can see our dissatisfaction with our breasts, our stomachs, or our cellulite, but we can't see our partners' passion for us, and in so doing we undermine ourselves, our sexual pleasure, our lovers, and perhaps ultimately even our relationships. I am highlighting women's roles in these dynamics not to let men off the hook for the infractions they might commit, but rather to expose the ways we as women might be working against ourselves in relationships that are important to us.

HOW WE WANT IT TO BE DIFFERENT FOR OUR DAUGHTERS

When asked what they hoped their daughters' relationship to body image would be like, women said things like: *I really hope to not put the kind of pressure on her that my mother put on me. I would hope that she can accept herself as is, and try to be healthy, not "perfect."* And, *I hope that my daughter has unconditional love for herself (including body image). To be at peace with yourself and grateful for what you have is an extremely powerful gift.*

Intellectually, we understand that we should raise our daughters to have subjective ownership over their bodies. But the emotional/ psychological question we have to ask ourselves is: Why would our daughters *want* to take subjective ownership over what they've been taught by us to disdain?

The women who completed the body image questionnaire also had the opportunity to give voice to their hopes for themselves by responding to the following question: "If the importance placed on having the perfect body vanished, what would you like to be most valued for as a woman?" More than 60 percent wanted to be valued for their intelligence, with compassion running a close second.

We can use that intelligence and compassion we value so highly in ourselves to instruct our daughters' development of the same.

Conclusion

*I*t's my hope that this book will be of benefit to mothers not only on the personal level, but on the cultural level as well, because as we contribute to our own mother-daughter relationships, so do we contribute to redefining the mother-daughter relationship in general. My intention has been to provide a fresh examination of the mother-daughter bond and to offer things we can do to make it healthier and stronger, so that we both feel freer to thrive. If collectives of mothers approach this objective together, the cultural water-level will rise and we can have a hand in making our society healthier and stronger. Trying to end sexism by bringing about gender equality is a daunting objective. Each of us is only one mother. But what percentage of our culture do mothers represent? And when we recognize how much influence we have over both our daughters' and our sons' perspective on female sexuality, how far does our sphere of influence extend?

The first wave of feminism set us on a course of winning *fundamental rights.* The second wave, in addition to continuing to procure rights, won us more freedom to find *our selves.* I believe that the third wave, as it furthers the expansion of equal rights, should also involve *reaching for our daughters, and bringing them forward with us*—not only in envisioning their theoretical futures, such as anticipating that they will vote at 18, but in the aliveness of the present, by nourishing their right to human sexuality and body integrity from the time they're little.

Mothers have an opportunity to protect this human right using a tremendous amount of autonomy. We can do it without needing the approval of the U.S. Supreme Court, the aid of law enforcement, without relying on the fairness of corporate culture, or the vagaries of insurance coverage. Its success isn't dependent on winning an election, raising capital, or organizing marches. This cultural change can be worked on naturally, through the simple freedoms we bestow upon our daughters and ourselves in the private intimacies of the mother-daughter bond—during our bedtime tuck-ins, on our walks, in our kitchens, and in our listening.

All of the issues presented in this book are incredibly complex, and I fully understand that neither I, nor any other single person or discipline of study, has all the answers. But because sexuality holds such a special place in the triumvirate of mental, emotional, and physical health, tending to its development in the home, where the sense of who we are in the world is shaped, is a rich, arable place to begin.

We need to be conscious of the ways we inadvertently deaden our daughters and each other with our silence and shame. We need instead to cultivate openness and respect for who we are as individuals—to embrace our sexual subjectivity, the thrum of our desire, and an unencumbered ability to live in our bodies as we see fit. And we need to do this as our men and boys bear witness and take it into their consciousness. We most especially need to be generous with our young. Our daughters will be up against enough in this world; they don't need to be undermined by their own gender. We should try to shepherd them into their sexuality, because the reality is, they're not just girls. They are women in the making. Trying to keep them as girls—and by that I mean tamping or denying their sexual vibrancy in an attempt to keep them underground as a sexual class—is what is at the root of sexism. We should try to take care not to commit the very same crime against them, ourselves and each other.

Sending our daughters out into the world with the understanding that we want them to be true to their minds, their hearts, and their bodies should be an honor. Whatever we wish for them as they face womanhood is what we should wish for ourselves; and whatever we privately wish for ourselves we should want for the next generation of women.

Nurturing the sexual integrity of our daughters is far from something to fear. It is an ongoing and enduring act of maternal love.

Appendix A

Women's Realities Study Questionnaire Topics

LIFE TRANSITIONS	RELATIONSHIPS	SEXUALITY
• Menstruation • Pregnancy • Childbirth • Perimenopause • Menopause • Postmenopause • Aging • Grief	• With your mother • With your father • With your sister(s) • With your brother(s) • With childhood girlfriends • With adult girlfriends • With men	• Masturbation • Orgasm • Loss of virginity • Sexuality in adolescence • Sexuality in the single woman • Sexuality in the married woman/ woman in long-term relationship
LOVE RELATIONSHIPS / GOOD & BAD	**MOTHERING**	**VIOLENCE AGAINST WOMEN/GIRLS**
• Marriage • Long-term committed relationships without marriage • Affairs • Separation • Divorce	• Being a mother • Being a stepmother • Being a grandmother/ great-grandmother • Relationship with your daughter(s) • Relationship with your son(s) • Adoption	• Sexual abuse • Physical abuse • Rape • Verbal Abuse • Sexual harassment

SINGLE WOMEN	CAREER/ EMPLOYMENT	LESBIANS/ BISEXUALS
• Single women	• Career/ employment	• Lesbians/ bisexuals
MENTAL AND PHYSICAL HEALTH	**FERTILITY/ INFERTILITY**	**WOMEN WHO HAVE NOT HAD CHILDREN**
• Depression • Anxiety • Eating disorders • Alcohol and substance abuse • Postpartum depression • Heart disease • Female cancers • AIDS/HIV • Sexually transmitted diseases • Gynecological conditions	• Abortion pre-Roe v. Wade • Abortion post-Roe v. Wade • Miscarriage • Stillborn baby • Giving up baby for adoption • Assisted reproduction	• Inability to have children • Not having children by choice
APPEARANCE	**WRAP UP**	
• Physical appearance • Body image • Medical procedures • Thoughts on the marketing of beauty	• *4 Final Questions Before Survey Completion*	

Appendix B

Questionnaire: Menstruation

5.   What did you know about menstruation before you started?

6.   Who, if anyone, taught you about it? (check all that apply)

- ☐ mother
- ☐ father
- ☐ stepmother
- ☐ stepfather
- ☐ grandmother
- ☐ aunt
- ☐ sister
- ☐ other relative
- ☐ girlfriend
- ☐ school nurse
- ☐ other
- ☐ no one

---

* Please note that each of the answer fields for women to write in was open-ended. Even though it isn't visually apparent in how the questionnaires appear in these appendices, the fields expanded to accommodate as much as each woman wanted to say.

7. Describe both what was explained to you, and how it was explained, verbally, biologically, and emotionally.

8. Do you wish it had been handled differently? If so, how, and by whom?

9. Please describe in detail the emotional and physical experience of your first period.

10. If you did know something of menstruation before you got your first period, how did what you imagined it would be differ from the reality?

11. Looking back on your first period now, what are your thoughts?

12. What form of sanitary feminine protection do you use, and is there anything you would do to improve upon it to make it better, more comfortable, more convenient, etc.?

13. How would you describe the level and quality of pain or discomfort during your period, and has it changed over the years?

14. How would you describe the level and quality of changes in your emotional state during your period, and has it changed over the years?

15. Have you had serious complications or chronic medical conditions in your cycle? If so please explain.

16. If you have, or imagine having, a daughter, how did you or would you explain menstruation to her?

17. At what age would you explain it to her?
☐ 6
☐ 7
☐ 8
☐ 9
☐ 10
☐ 11
☐ 12
☐ 13
☐ 14
☐ 15
☐ 16
☐ 17
☐ never

18. How would you describe your relationship with menstruation as you look over the years?

19. Is there a menstrual experience that stands out to you? If so, please describe it and its significance.

20. How have the men in your life responded to your cycle?

21. If men menstruated instead of women, how do you imagine things would be different? Please describe in full detail.

22. DEMOGRAPHIC INFORMATION: Your age:

23. Race

☐ Asian
☐ African American
☐ Caucasian
☐ Hispanic
☐ Other

20. Race: If other, please specify

```



```

21. Sexual orientation

☐ Bisexual
☐ Heterosexual
☐ Homosexual

22. Religion

☐ Catholic
☐ Jewish
☐ Protestant
☐ Other

23. Religion: If other, please specify

```



```

24. Education

☐ Some high school
☐ High school graduate
☐ Some college
☐ College graduate
☐ Some graduate school
☐ Graduate school graduate
☐ Postgraduate

25. Marital status

☐ Single
☐ Living together
☐ Married
☐ Divorced
☐ Widowed

26. Career/employment (including mothering)

27. State of residence

Appendix C

Questionnaire:
Relationship with Your Mother

IF YOUR MOTHER IS DECEASED, PLEASE RESPOND TO YOUR RELATIONSHIP WHEN SHE WAS ALIVE.

1. Would you describe your relationship with your mother as: (check all that apply)

☐ fabulous
☐ good and strictly mother-daughter
☐ good and somewhat girl-friendy
☐ good and strictly girl-friendy
☐ a role reversal--I mothered her
☐ close but mediocre
☐ distant and mediocre
☐ bad
☐ turbulent
☐ a nightmare
☐ so complex it defies categorization

2. What is the quality of your relationship that draws you the closest to her, and why is this what stands out to you?

3. What is the quality of your relationship that pushes you farthest away from her, and why is this what stands out to you?

4. What do you most admire in your mother?

5. What do you want her to most admire in you?

6. What is your deepest regret as a daughter?

7. What do you believe should be your mother's deepest regret as a mother?

8. How do you feel when your mother hugs you?

9. What do you want to know about your mother but would never ask?

10. What keeps you from asking?

11. Do you feel that when you're with your mother you are more expansive or more diminutive?

12. Please describe the feelings that influenced your response to the previous question.

13. Do you feel your mother really knows you, really gets who you are?

14. Do you feel you really know, really get who your mother is?

15. If your mother was cruel to you in some way, how do you process this emotionally?

16. Do you ever feel like a misfit in your family in that if it weren't for being related you would never choose to spend time with your mother?

17. How has your relationship with your mother changed from when you were a child to now as an adult?

18. What percentage of you uses your mother as a role model for how to move through your life as a woman? (check one)

- ☐ less than 20 percent
- ☐ 21–30 percent
- ☐ 41–50 percent
- ☐ 51–60 percent
- ☐ 61–70 percent
- ☐ 71–80 percent
- ☐ 81–90 percent
- ☐ 91–100 percent

19. What personality trait of your mother's do you have that you love or respect? What is the quality that makes this trait stand out to you?

20. What personality trait of your mother's do you have that you hate or disrespect? What is the quality that makes this trait stand out to you?

21. Please describe the nature of the most complex facet of your relationship with your mother and how the two of you attempt to navigate this.

22. What do you want others to know about your experience of your relationship with your mother?

Appendix D

Questionnaire:
Masturbation

1. Do you masturbate? (check one)
☐ yes
☐ no

2. If not, please explain why this is the case.

+--+
| |
| |
| |
| |
| |
+--+

3. When do you tend to masturbate? In what state of mind or mood? What is usually going on for you in the moments before?

+--+
| |
| |
| |
| |
| |
+--+

4. What do you hope to feel, physically and emotionally, during and after? How long would you say this process usually takes?

+--+
| |
| |
| |
| |
| |
+--+

5. Does masturbation feel more about physical sensation or fantasy, or a combination of both? Please describe.

6. Do you and your women friends ever discuss masturbation? If so, how would you describe these conversations? If not, why do you believe this is, and do you wish masturbation was a topic women openly discussed?

7. Do you experience guilt around masturbation? (check one)
   ☐ yes
   ☐ no

8. If so, what do you believe warrants the guilt?

9. If you do not experience guilt, please elaborate.

```




```

10. Is there anything, physical or emotional, that you feel during masturbation that you wish you felt during sex? Please describe.

```




```

11. How would you describe the difference in experience between masturbation and sex? Do you prefer one over the other, and if so, why?

```




```

12. Did anyone ever teach you about masturbation as a normal aspect of human sexuality? (check one)

☐ yes

☐ no

13. If not, what do you wish such a conversation would have been like?

14. If you have, or imagine having, a daughter, would you explain masturbation to her? (check one)
- [ ] yes
- [ ] no At what age? (check one)
- [ ] 6–8
- [ ] 9–11
- [ ] 12–14
- [ ] 15–17
- [ ] 18–20
- [ ] older than 20
- [ ] never

15. Please explain why you would or would not tell her.

16. How do you typically masturbate, and what are the qualities of this experience, physically and emotionally, that make it your preferred way?

17. How did you feel responding to these questions? How do you imagine other women responding to this survey felt?

18. If this survey were to be published, would you be interested in hearing other women's thoughts and feelings about masturbation? Why, or why not?

Notes

INTRODUCTION A CAUTIONARY TALE

1. Carol Gilligan, "Love and Diane," *Point of View*, PBS, April 21, 2004.

2. Barbara F. Marcus, "Female Passion and the Matrix of Mother, Daughter, and Body: Vicissitudes of the Maternal Transference in the Working" through of Sexual Inhibitions," *Psychoanalytic Inquiry* 24, no. 5 (November 2004): 680–712.

3. A list of all questionnaire topics can be found in Appendix A.

4. *UNICEF Innocenti Report Card*, July 2001.

5. American Academy of Child and Adolescent Psychiatry, *Talking to Your Kids about Sex* (2005).

6. American Academy of Pediatrics, *Talking to Your Young Child about Sex* (December 11, 2009).

7. Justin Richardson and Mark A. Schuster, *Everything You Never Wanted Your Kids to Know About Sex (but Were Afraid They'd Ask)* (New York: Three Rivers Press, 2003).

8. Deborah Tolman, *Dilemmas of Desire: Teenage Girls Talk about Sexuality* (Cambridge, MA: Harvard University Press, 2002).

9. Naomi Wolf, *Promiscuities: The Secret Struggle for Womanhood* (New York: Ballantine, 1998).

10. Debra Haffner, *Beyond the Big Talk* (New York: Newmarket Press, 2001).

11. *Oprah*, March 26, 2009.

CHAPTER ONE HOW OUR MOTHERS INFLUENCE US

1. Irene P. Stiver, "Beyond the Oedipus Complex: Mothers and Daughters," *Stone Center Colloquium*, May 7, 1986.

2. Daniel Bergner, "What Is Female Desire?" *The New York Times Magazine*, January 25, 2009.

3. Jessica Benjamin, *The Bonds of Love: Psychoanalysis, Feminism, and the Problem of Domination* (New York: Pantheon Books, 1988), p. 90.

4. Daniel N. Stern, *The Interpersonal World of the Infant: A View from Psychoanalysis and Developmental Psychology* (New York: Basic Books, 1985), p. 38.

5. Alison Gopnik, *The Philosophical Baby: What Children's Minds Tell Us About Truth, Love, and the Meaning of Life* (New York: Picador, 2009), pp. 81, 205.

6. These questions were designed for the book—they were informed by, but not part of the study.

7. *Oprah*, April 10, 2009.

8. Esther Perel, *Mating in Captivity* (New York: HarperCollins, 2006), p. 151.

9. Stephen A. Mitchell, *Relational Concepts in Psychoanalysis: An Integration* (Cambridge, MA: Harvard University Press, 1988), p. 148.

10. Nathalie Bartle, *Venus in Blue Jeans: Why Mothers and Daughters Need to Talk about Sex* (New York: Dell Publishing, 1998), p. 181.

11. American Academy of Child and Adolescent Psychiatry, *Talking to Your Kids about Sex* (2005).

12. American Academy of Pediatrics, *Talking to Your Young Child about Sex* (December 11, 2009).

CHAPTER TWO ARE YOU THERE, MOM? IT'S ME, YOUR DAUGHTER

1. Mary Pipher, *Reviving Ophelia* (New York: Random House, 1994), p. 53.

2. J. E. Tangney, "Conceptual and Methodological Issues in the Assessment of Shame and Guilt," *Behaviour Research & Therapy* 34, no. 9 (September 1996): 743.

3. Barbara Marcus, "Female Passion and the Matrix of Mother, Daughter, and Body: Vicissitudes of the Maternal Transference in the Working through of Sexual Inhibitions," *Psychoanalytic Inquiry* 24, no. 5 (November 2004): 680–712.

4. Deborah Schooler, L. Monique Ward, Ann Merriweather, Allison S. Caruthers, "Cycles of Shame: Menstrual Shame, Body Shame, and Sexual Decision-Making," *Journal of Sex Research* (November 2005).

5. Phyllis Tyson, "Bedrock and Beyond: An Examination of the Clinical Utility of Contemporary Theories of Female Psychology," *Journal of the American Psychoanalytic Association* 42, no. 2 (1994): 447–67.

6. Heinz Kohut, *The Search for the Self: Selected Writings of Heinz Kohut, 1950–1981*. 4 vols. (New York: International University Press, 1988–1991).

7. D. DeMarneffe, "Bodies and Words: A Study of Young Children's Genital and Gender Knowledge," *Gender and Psychoanalysis* 2 (1997): 3–33.

8. Justin Richardson and Mark A. Schuster, *Everything You Never Wanted Your Kids to Know About Sex (but Were Afraid They'd Ask)* (New York: Three Rivers Press, 2003), p. 87.

9. *The G. Gordon Liddy Show*, Radio America, May 20, 2008.

10. Barbara Berg, *Sexism in America: Alive, Well, and Ruining Our Future* (Chicago: Lawrence Hill Books, 2009), p. 154.

11. Deborah L. Tolman, *Dilemmas of Desire: Teenage Girls Talk about Sexuality* Cambridge, MA: Harvard University Press, 2002), p. 6.

12. T. A. Roberts, "Female Trouble: The Menstrual Self-Evaluation Scale and Women's Self-Objectification," *Psychology of Women Quarterly* 28, no. 10 (2004): 22–26.

13. Robie H. Harris, *It's Perfectly Normal: Changing Bodies, Growing Up, Sex and Sexual Health* (Cambridge, MA: Candlewick Press, 2004).

14. Schooler et al., "Cycles of Shame."

15. Ashley Montagu, *The Natural Superiority of Women* (New York: Macmillan, 1952), p. 32.

16. Ibid., p. 18.

17. Ibid, p. 22.

18. Alexandra Jacobs, "There Will Be Blood," *The New York Times*, March 12, 2009.

19. Clara Thompson, "Cultural Pressures in the Psychology of Women," *Psychiatry* 5 (1942): 331–39.

CHAPTER THREE LETTING OUR DAUGHTERS SEE US AS SEXUAL WOMEN

1. Justin Richardson and Mark A. Schuster, *Everything You Never Wanted Your Kids to Know About Sex (but Were Afraid They'd Ask)* (New York: Three Rivers Press, 2003), p. 113.

2. Natalie L. Dove and Michael W. Weiderman, "Cognitive Distraction and Women's Sexual Functioning," *Journal of Sex and Marital Therapy* 26 (2000): 67–78.

3. Alfred C. Kinsey et al., *Sexual Behavior in the Human Female* (Philadelphia: W. B. Saunders, 1953).

4. William H. Masters and Virginia E. Johnson, *Human Sexual Response* (Boston: Little, Brown, 1966).

5. Betty Dodson, *Sex for One: The Joy of Selfloving* (New York: Three Rivers Press, 1996); Jayme Waxman, *Getting Off: A Woman's Guide to Masturbation* (Berkeley: Seal Press, 2007).

6. Christiane Northrup, *The Wisdom of Menopause* (New York: Bantam, 2001).

7. Jennifer Berman and Laura Berman, *For Women Only: A Revolutionary Guide to Reclaiming Your Sex Life* (New York: Henry Holt, 2001).

8. Roy J. Levin, "Sexual Activity, Health and Well-Being—The Beneficial Roles of Coitus and Masturbation," *Sexual and Relationship Therapy* 22, no. 1 (February 2007); Department of Biomedical Science, University of Sheffield, Western Bank, Sheffield, UK, PorterBrook Clinic, Sheffield, UK.

9. Barry Komisaruk and Barbara Whipple, *The Science of Orgasm* (Baltimore, MD: Johns Hopkins University Press, 2006).

10. Sigmund Freud, "A Case of Obsessional Neurosis," in D. Wedding and R. J. Corsini (eds.), *Great Cases in Psychotherapy* (Itaska, IL: F. E. Peacock, 1979), p. 27.

11. Peter Pearce and Valerie Simanowitz, *Personality Development* (Maidenhead, Berkshire, England: McGraw Hill, 2003).

12. Daniel Bergner, "What Is Female Desire?" *The New York Times Magazine*, January 25, 2009.

13. American Academy of Pediatrics, Healthy Children website, http://www. healthychildren.org/English/Pages/default.aspx.

14. Richardson and Schuster, *Everything You Never Wanted Your Kids to Know about Sex*, p. 17.

15. Deborah M. Roffman, *Sex and Sensibility: The Thinking Parent's Guide to Talking Sense about Sex* (Cambridge, MA: DaCapo Press, 2001), p 171.

16. Deborah L. Tolman, *Dilemmas of Desire: Teenage Girls Talk about Sexuality* (Cambridge, MA: Harvard University Press, 2002), p. 129.

17. Ibid., p. 60.

18. Ibid.

19. Nathalie Bartle, *Venus in Blue Jeans: Why Mothers and Daughters Need to Talk about Sex* (New York: Dell, 1998), p. 70.

20. Ibid., pp. 163–164.

21. Esther Perel, *Mating in Captivity* (New York: HarperCollins, 2006), p. 57.

22. Harriet Hogart and Roger Ingham, "Masturbation among Young Women and Associations with Sexual Health: An Exploratory Study," *Journal of Sex Research* 46 (2009): 1–10.

23. Laura Kipnis, *The Female Thing* (New York: Pantheon Books, 2006), pp. 44–45.

24. Sarah Tofte, "Lost Promise for Rape Victims," *Los Angeles Times*, June 30, 2008.

25. U.S. Department of Health and Human Services, *Administration for Children and Families, and Child Welfare Information Gateway Reports*, 2008.

26. Susan J. Douglas, *Enlightened Sexism: The Seductive Message That Feminism's Work Is Done* (New York: Henry Holt, 2010), p. 13.

27. Ibid., p. 14.

28. Ibid., p. 184.

29. Simone de Beauvoir, *The Second Sex* (New York: Knopf, 1952), p. 517.

30. John Donne, "Death Be Not Proud," *The Norton Anthology of English Literature*, 4th ed. (New York: W. W. Norton, 1979), p. 1101.

CHAPTER FOUR THE LIFELONG CONVERSATION WITH OUR DAUGHTERS ABOUT SEXUALITY

1. American Academy of Child and Adolescent Psychiatry, *Talking to Your Kids about Sex* (2005).

2. Nathalie Bartle, *Venus in Blue Jeans: Why Mothers and Daughters Need to Talk about Sex* (New York: Dell Publishing, 1998), p. 156.

3. "What I've Learned," *Esquire*, January 2003.

4. Harriet Hogarth and Roger Ingham, "Masturbation among Young Women and Associations with Sexual Health: An Exploratory Study," *Journal of Sex Research* 46 (2009): 1–10.

CHAPTER FIVE WHAT DO YOU MOST WANT TO KNOW ABOUT YOUR MOTHER BUT WOULD NEVER ASK?

1. M. Yalom, S. Estler, and W. Brewster, "Changes in Female Sexuality: A Study of Mother/Daughter Communication and Generational Differences." *Psychology of Women Quarterly*, vol. 7, no. 2 (Winter 1982): 50.

2. J. Benjamin, *The Bonds of Love: Psychoanalysis, Feminism, and the Problem of Domination* (New York: Pantheon Books, 1988), p. 98.

3. Deborah Tolman, *Dilemmas of Desire: Teenage Girls Talk about Sexuality* (Cambridge, MA: Harvard University Press, 2002), p. 20.

4. RAINN.org, *National Crime Victimization Survey*, 2004.

CHAPTER SIX SAVING OUR DAUGHTERS FROM OUR BEST INTENTIONS

1. Jeffrey Zaslow, "Girls Dieting, Then and Now," *Wall Street Journal*, September 2, 2009.

2. Randi Hutter Epstein, "When Eating Disorders Strike in Midlife," *The New York Times*, July 13, 2009.

Index